A Guide to Minnesota's Oldest State Park

The *Best* of Itasca

by Deane Johnson

Adventure Publications
Cambridge, Minnesota

Dedication

This book is dedicated to my wife, Jill Johnson, fellow writer, hiker and lifelong inspiration.

Acknowledgments

Sincere thanks to all who helped in some way with this book—even the smallest contribution is valuable in such a diverse project. Chelsey Johnson for expert editorial assistance and guidance; Kara Thompson, Nate Johnson, Dan Johnson, Ann Grace and Jim Musburger for your encouragement and editorial help; Leif Johnson, our hope for the future. Special thanks to all Itasca State Park and regional DNR staff for your cooperation and expertise. To all who helped with photos and information: Park Rapids Library staff; fellow flower-seekers Trista Little, Ellen Folman, Jessica Stuber-Benzie; Frank Mitchell; LuAnn Hurd-Lof, Katie Magozzi and Park Rapids Chamber of Commerce; CCC Group, Leroy and Louise Czeczok, Murl and Kathy McGrane, Dorothy Welle, Don and Helen Tschudi, Ren Holland; Tamara Edevold and Clearwater County Historical Society; Marvin Henderson, Connie Henderson and Hubbard County Historical Society; Dan Karalus and Beltrami County Historical Society; Pat Evenwoll of Bert's Cabins; Rory Palm and Park Rapids Enterprise; Bill Thoma; Minnesota Historical Society; Bemidji State University Library; University of Minnesota Library; Paul Peterson, Brita Sailer, Dale Sheldon, Tim Holzkamm, Lyle Colligan, Dick Sauer, Dorothy, Jack and Linda Katzenmeyer, Leonard Hemmerich; tireless trail and bike companions Mike and Jacque McCann, Guy and Cathy Reich, Mark and Barb Thomason, Terry and Kathy Dunklee, Royce and Kathy Peterson, Maurice and Carolyn Spangler, Bill and Donna Neumann, Ray Niedzielski, Mike and Sandy Perez, Mike and Janine Wiedemann, Kevin and Renee Brauer, Rob and Mary Beth Anderson; North Country Trail crew and friends Bruce Johnson, Carter Hedeen, Darrel Rodekuhr, Ray Vlasak, Susan Carol Hauser; photography advisors Joel Maxwell, Steve Maanum, Neil King, Cal Rice, Steve Peterson, Richard Hamilton Smith, Dave Shogren; Marshall Howe for sharing your love of birds; Dick Kimball for last-minute changes. Forgive me if I forgot you—everyone's help made a difference. Special thanks to Gerri and Gordon Slabaugh, Brett Ortler, Jonathan Norberg, and everyone at Adventure Publications for your expert work and creativity. It is an understatement to say that I couldn't have done it without you.

Researching the history of the development of Itasca State Park would have been immeasurably more difficult without Jacob V. Brower's two works, *The Mississippi and its Source*, and *Itasca State Park: An Illustrated History*. Brower's tireless and generous work in establishing Itasca State Park in the face of fierce opposition should inspire all who attempt to follow in his footsteps. His books were used as a source throughout the book, as was John Dobie's *The Itasca Story*, published in 1959.

Illustrations by Jonathan Norberg
Cover and book design by Jonathan Norberg
Front and back cover photos by Deane Johnson
Photo credits listed on page 271.

Table of Contents

Introduction

My earliest memory of Itasca State Park is of buffalo. We were at a family picnic in the park sometime in the 1950s, and I saw the buffalo pens nearby. As I looked through that woven wire fence at the shaggy beasts a few feet away, they seemed so powerful and the fence so frail; I feared they might easily plow through it at will. That short visit to the bison was enough for me, and I was more than happy to return to the picnic grounds and then walk over the rocks on the mighty Mississippi.

Growing up on the prairie of Grand Forks, North Dakota, leaves one with a longing for trees and hills, so the lake country of northern Minnesota was always a dream. As I grew older, a few days of fishing and exploring the backwaters of Itasca lakes was exciting, but the Dr. Roberts Trail provided my first real introduction to the special wonders of Itasca State Park. On a Memorial Day walk around that trail with my wife, Jill, and our friends from Bad Medicine Lake, Mike and Shirleen, we saw flowers and trees that I had never seen before in the Red River Valley. Small yellow lady's slippers, bunchberry and false lily-of-the-valley were in full bloom, and strange ferns, lichens and feathery horsetail rushes were everywhere.

Those experiences forged a bond that has never been broken, and the park's proximity was a deciding factor in our decision to move to Park Rapids a few years later. Since then we have learned the joys of skiing and snowshoeing under the big pines, biking around Wilderness Drive, hiking the trails, and of course, teetering over the rocks at the Headwaters, and sharing all of this with family and friends. My affection for and understanding of Itasca State Park has deepened since I took a Master Naturalist course here in 2011 and began volunteer work to help restore plant identification on Dr. Roberts Trail, the same trail that had captivated me decades earlier.

In 2011 my wife Jill wrote *Little Minnesota: 100 Towns Around 100*, for which I did the photography. After that project had been published, I began work on what I thought would be a simple guide to the hiking trails of Itasca. I soon realized that this area has been deeply intertwined with human history for thousands of years, beginning with the ancestors of today's Dakota and Ojibwe. Itasca State Park was established in 1891, shortly after the first European immigrants began settling in this part of the state in the 1870s. When I first read

Jacob V. Brower's books in the Park Rapids library years ago, I was riveted by his vivid story and the bitter struggle to establish Itasca State Park in the face of powerful competing interests of his day. His story made it clear that changes due to logging, settlement, the growth of towns and cities, agriculture, and everything good and bad that go with them, are all part of the story of Itasca State Park.

My goals for this book are first to provide a detailed trail guide, so that hikers and skiers can choose which trails they might like and enjoy the historic and natural highlights as they go. I have also described a selection of the plants, animals and birds that all live here, so the reader can consider how they live together, and how human activity impacts the natural systems at work. With hundreds of years of oral history and hundreds of birds, flowers, trees and animals to consider, this work is a sampler of a much larger picture. I have tried to hit the high points, with the hope that you will be inspired to dig further into field guides, history books and other resources.

So come to Itasca, walk over the Headwaters, climb the tower and do everything that every Itasca visitor loves to do. Then try some of the trails less traveled. Stop and look down for the tiny flowers you've been missing, listen for birds that you may not hear in the big city, smell the balsam fir and pines, and let nature do its work of enriching your life.

"Nature is not a place to visit. It is home."
—Gary Snyder, *The Etiquette of Freedom*

Wilderness Drive

Best of Itasca!

"What err' Itasca means to thee, to me it stands for peace and rest. The sound of the wind in the pines, and the scent of sun kissed balsam."

Mrs. J. E. Wallis, St. Paul. Douglas Lodge Guest Book, August 4, 1921

Itasca State Park has 50 miles of hiking trails, 16 miles of bike routes, 28 miles of skiing trails, 32 miles of snowmobiling trails, 100 lakes, and dozens of beautiful historic buildings to explore, all within 32,836 acres of pine and hardwood forests that are up to 300 years old. With all of that to see and do, it's hard to know where to begin. That's why I've compiled a list of my nine favorite sights and activities at the park. When I bring friends and family to visit the park, this is where I take them first.

Aiton Heights Fire Tower view of Clarke Lake

HERE 1475 FT
ABOVE
THE OCEAN
THE MIGHTY
MISSISSIPPI
BEGINS
TO FLOW
ON ITS
WINDING WAY
2552 MILES
TO THE
GULF OF
MEXICO

Headwaters of the Mississippi

Jacob V. Brower Visitor Center

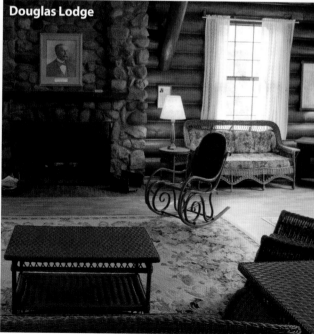

Douglas Lodge

Headwaters of the Mississippi

Most people begin right here, at the Headwaters, and some come to Itasca just to cross the rocks over the Mississippi River. The Ojibwe named it *gitchi-ziibi*, meaning "great river." Don't be disappointed to learn that the Civilian Conservation Corps (CCC) reshaped the outlet and placed those rocks over a dam in the 1930s. When the CCC boys rearranged the outlet, they used a 1901 map, restoring the river to the course it originally followed before loggers had straightened it to sluice logs through the narrow channel. Hopefully you will have more time to see the rest of the park, but if not, this is many visitors' first and favorite site and their most vivid memory of the park. The Headwaters Trail begins at Mary Gibbs Mississippi Headwaters Center near the North Entrance to the park and is a level, ADA-accessible walk of 800 feet, which is kept open in the winter, though it is not as accessible. The Mary Gibbs Center canopy shelters outdoor displays and a 20-foot-long, three-dimensional table map of the Mississippi River, available for year-round use. The visitor center's large gift shop and cafeteria are open Memorial Day weekend through early fall.

Jacob V. Brower Visitor Center

This relatively new facility, located just inside the East Entrance, is your one stop for information about anything related to Itasca State Park. A cozy lounge area with two modern fireplaces welcomes you and is open after hours during skiing season. You can find maps, general information about the park and surrounding area, interpretive and hands-on displays, videos and detailed trail condition reports. A large classroom hosts indoor naturalist programs, educational events, and meetings. The park's naturalist programs are a highlight, especially for new visitors to the area, and there is a special emphasis on programming for children of all ages.

Douglas Lodge

As beautiful and inspiring today as it was when it was dedicated in 1905, Douglas Lodge was built in the Rustic Style popular in national parks of that era. It has been updated and changed over the years to accommodate modern lodging and food-service standards but still retains the look and feel of the day it was first completed. The dining room has excellent food, which is focused on Minnesota cuisine, such as wild rice soup and casseroles, blueberry malts, bison burgers, and an exclusively Minnesota wine and beer list.

Forest Inn

Aiton Heights Fire Tower

Lake Itasca Swimming Beach

Wilderness Drive

Forest Inn

Built by the Veterans Conservation Corps in 1938, this flagship of the 1930s Itasca State Park buildings has a modern gift shop, a large gathering area with a grand fireplace, and a lobby with fine woodwork that looks much as it did when it was constructed. Edward Barber and V. C. Martin, architects from the Minnesota Central Design Office of the National Park Service, designed the Forest Inn and other Itasca State Park buildings of the 1930s. Their influence is seen in other Minnesota and National Park Service structures of that era.

Aiton Heights Fire Tower

Climb a securely enclosed metal stairway to the top of the 100-foot tower to see the park as fire spotters saw it in the 1940s. This is especially popular from mid-September to early October, as leaves splash the landscape with reds and yellows against a backdrop of green pines. To get there, you can walk less than half a mile uphill from the parking lot off Wilderness Drive, or hike 3 miles round-trip from Douglas Lodge.

Picnic Grounds and Swimming Beach

Itasca's beautiful picnic grounds stretch along a wide area of Lake Itasca's shore and have been the site for family gatherings and group picnics since the park's earliest days. The picnic grounds also include a small history museum, an outdoor performance space, a replica of a 1930s picnic shelter, and a wide, sandy beach with a volleyball court and CCC-era changing house built from logs and stone.

Wilderness Drive

It is said that many visitors come for the Headwaters but return for the pines. This 16-mile-plus round-trip, beginning on Main Park Drive or the bike trail, and then looping around Wilderness Drive, is one of the most beautiful biking and driving routes in the state. Wilderness Drive provides a contrast in tree cover, with 100-year-old hardwoods and younger pines in the logged-over areas and up to 300-year-old red and white pine stands in the Itasca Wilderness Sanctuary. It also leads to most of the popular hiking trails of all lengths and difficulty levels, including the Aiton Heights Fire Tower Trail.

Lake Itasca Boat Landing

Brower Trail

Boat Landing

Rent a boat, canoe or kayak and do some fishing, or just paddle around for a closer look at Schoolcraft Island, water birds and the wild lakeshore, with its reeds, lily pads and extensive wild rice beds.

Hiking

With 50 miles of hiking trails, Itasca has some great hiking to offer. These particular trails are well worth visiting. If you're interested in short, easy hikes (up to 0.5 mile), try out the Maadaadizi Trail (page 97), the first section of the Dr. Roberts Trail (page 86), the Big Red Pine and Big White Pine Trails (page 70) or the Landmark Trail, an interpretive trail (page 93).

For a moderately difficult hike (1–3 miles), there are many options. You can take the Nicollet Trail (page 103), the Aiton Heights loop (page 66) or the Schoolcraft Trail (page 124). Beginning near the Headwaters, the Schoolcraft is a birder's favorite. The Dr. Roberts Trail (page 86) features plant and tree identification; pick up an interpretive guidebook at Jacob V. Brower Visitor Center or Forest Inn. Check out the old-growth pines of the Bohall Trail (page 74), or visit the Brower Trail (page 76), which boasts several access points to the lake and a number of historic sites.

Overview Map

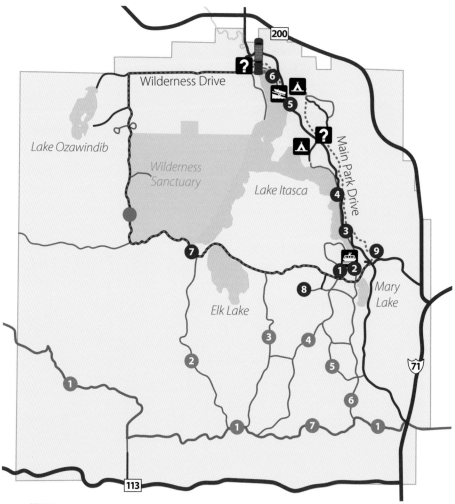

KEY

1. Douglas Lodge
2. Forest Inn
3. Preacher's Grove
4. Peace Pipe Vista
5. Hostel
6. Beach, Picnic Grounds, Museum
7. Bison Kill Site
8. Aiton Heights Fire Tower
9. Jacob V. Brower Visitor Center

- Bike Trail
1. North Country Trail
2. Nicollet Trail
3. DeSoto Trail
4. Deer Park Trail
5. Red Pine Trail
6. Ozawindib Trail
7. Eagle Scout Trail

A Guide to Itasca

This section includes travel routes to the park, lodging, activities and other essentials to consider when you plan your trip.

The second-largest state park in Minnesota, Itasca State Park covers an amazing 47 square miles. With a park that large, it's often hard to know where to start. Look no further: this is your guide to visiting Itasca State Park. Here you'll find everything from lodging and camping details to a rundown of the park's many amenities and activities.

Budd Lake

Iron Corner Camp

Planning Your Trip

LOCATION

Located in north-central Minnesota, Itasca State Park is the crown jewel of the Minnesota State Parks system. Surrounded by vast expanses of wild forest and teeming with wildlife, the park is also home to dozens of lakes, including Lake Itasca, the Headwaters of the Mississippi River. Established in 1891, the park protects a remnant of the great pine forest that once covered much of northern Minnesota.

HOW TO GET THERE

US-71 approaches Itasca from Park Rapids to the south, US-71 and MN-200 come from Lake George and Bemidji to the east, and MN-200 and Clearwater County 2 lead in from the north. Through Delta Airlines, the Bemidji airport offers daily flights that connect to Minneapolis; Fargo (112 miles) and Minneapolis (220 miles) are the other major airports nearby. Car rental is available at these locations, but there is no regular public transportation to Itasca State Park. Take note that GPS directions often direct visitors to the South Entrance

Road, but it is closed in winter and groomed for skiing! In snowy months, enter via the East Entrance, on MN-200 just north of its junction with US-71, or via the North Entrance, 6 miles farther north on MN-200. For a guided driving tour of the park, see page 143.

SEASONS

Timing is everything in a visit to northern Minnesota. The temperature swings from an average high of 79 °F in July to an average low of -5 °F in January. Daytime temperatures are typically in the teens in January, but a cold air mass sinking down from Canada can keep the temperatures below zero for days at a time. The record low hit -52 °F in 1996. Spring begins in April as the snow melts and things begin to green up a bit, but the average high is only 52 °F and lows are typically subfreezing. By May, the average highs are 65 °F and trees are leafing out.

The weather and lake water temperatures warm to summer levels in June, the rainiest month of the year, but are usually unpredictable. July and August are the warmest months and often have stretches of stable warm weather interrupted by thunderstorms. September can be a beautiful and less busy time to see Itasca, with cooler evenings and fall color beginning mid-September and lasting into the first week of October. Mid-October through early December is a time of transition, when leaves are off the trees and bare ground is awaiting snow. Except for deer hunting (usually the first or second full week in November) it is a quiet time in the park, ideal for those seeking solitude. The cross-country skiing, snowshoeing and snowmobiling seasons begin whenever the snow builds up to a level that can cover the ground under the big pines, usually by late December, but sometimes later. The snow usually remains skiable until late February, or some years well into March, before the spring melt begins.

SAFETY

When visiting Itasca State Park, keep safety in mind. Wear bike helmets for biking, life jackets at all times when boating, and sunscreen and protective clothing in the sun. Mosquitoes are usually worse in the spring but can be pesky during any warm month, especially in the hours around sunset. A repellent may be needed to enjoy the outdoors at times. Ticks are active in all non-snowy months and are typically found on trail edges, woods and brush, and in tall grass. Unfortunately, ticks are more than a nuisance, as they can transmit disease. This is especially true for the smaller deer (blacklegged) ticks, which are most active in spring and late fall and can transmit nasty infections, such as Lyme disease and anaplasmosis (Ehrlichiosis). DEET repellents (20–30 percent maximum DEET) are somewhat effective for ticks, but products containing permethrin, which kill the ticks, are better. Permethrin should only be applied to camping gear, clothing or shoes and not directly to skin. DEET and permethrins should be applied with caution in all children, especially with infants. When hiking, tuck your pants into your socks and spray repellent on your clothing.

Also, keep your distance from wild animals. Food should be secured out of reach of bears and raccoons at backcountry campsites. Raccoons, though they look tame, are out for food, not companionship, and campground raccoons that have lost their fear of humans can get quite aggressive. Black bears live in Itasca State Park, but the bears rarely visit the campgrounds or backcountry campsites.

Douglas Lodge Cabin Interior

Lodging and Camping Options

Itasca State Park receives half a million visitors a year, so make lodging and camping reservations well in advance if you're planning on visiting during busy times of year, such as fishing opener in mid-May, the peak season from June through August, the fall colors season in late September, or the holiday weekends of Memorial Day, the Fourth of July and Labor Day. This is especially true for groups and tours.

Camping and lodging reservations can be made online up to a year in advance at the Minnesota State Park's site (http://www.dnr.state.mn.us/state_parks/reservations.html) or by calling (866) 857-2757. Not all camping sites are reservable, as some are available only on a first-come, first-served basis.

CAMPING
Bear Paw and Pine Ridge Campgrounds
Campers return year after year to camp among the tall pines of Itasca at Pine Ridge Campground or Bear Paw Campground, located near the Lake Itasca

shore. With 223 drive-in sites filled to the brim most summer weekends, the campgrounds can be busy and full of activity, although solitude is never too far away if you are able to get out on the trails. There are electric hookups at 160 of the campsites, with an RV length limit of 60 feet. Two sites in each campground are ADA-accessible, and so are the shower facilities, which are open early May through mid-October.

Pine Ridge Campground

Pine Ridge, on the site of the old Civilian Conservation Corps camp of the 1930s, has a majority of its campsites on roads that crisscross and loop the campground. Some of the campsites around the outside loop are tucked into the woods. The trees vary in age, with many of the younger ones dating back to the closing of the CCC camp in 1942. It is about a quarter-mile walk or bike ride down the hill to the boat landing; the swimming beach, museum and picnic grounds are a bit farther beyond. The LaSalle Trail, notable for big pines and lady's slippers, begins near the entrance to Pine Ridge Campground.

Bear Paw is located a bit farther south, above the Lake Itasca shoreline at the north end of Brower Trail. It has 70 drive-in sites for all campers and 11 cart-in sites for tent dwellers, with tent sites requiring a walk of up to 500 feet. There are six cabins available to rent; they have washrooms, but no showers, although renters can use the campground showers (see page 26).

The Campground Office serves both areas during the summer season and is located just off the Main Park Drive. In late fall, winter and early spring, contact the Jacob V. Brower Visitor Center, as just a portion of Pine Ridge Campground is operating. The campground map, available online or at the park, shows which sites can be reserved and gives a fairly good indication of the location and potential privacy (or lack thereof) of individual campsites.

Elk Lake Group Camp

Group Camps

Both the Elk Lake Group Camp and the Lake Ozawindib Group Center were the site of transient camps that were set up for unemployed workers during the CCC years. Today, they serve as group camps. Elk Lake Group Camp is the more basic of the two, with room for up to 50 people in tents, campers or RVs. It has vault toilets, a hand pump for water, and a small screened shelter. It is located near Elk Lake, a deep, clear lake that was claimed by some early explorers to be the true source of the Mississippi.

Lake Ozawindib Group Center has an indoor dining hall with air-conditioning and a commercial kitchen, a five-bed counselor cabin and a shower building. The group center can accommodate up to 75 campers, including school groups or adults, and is located in a secluded spot along Lake Ozawindib. Lake Ozawindib is in the western area of the park, which was added in 1919 after the land had been completely logged, and is now ringed by a maturing hardwood forest with some relatively young pines. (A separate road to the north side of the lake leads to the boat landing.) Lake Ozawindib Group Center was used as a recovery camp for Air Force personnel during World War II, but despite rumors to the contrary, never housed German prisoners of war.

Elk Lake Group Camp can be reserved online or by calling the toll-free reservation number (866) 857-2757. For Lake Ozawindib Group Center, call Itasca State Park directly at (218) 699-7251.

Backcountry Camping

Itasca has 11 backpacking campsites, and reaching them requires a walk ranging 1–5 miles. The sites can be reserved online or by phone, like the other campsites and lodging options. Backcountry camping should be reserved in advance if possible. Note that the website indicates that sites 2, 7 and 10 are first-come, first-served only, as is a North Country Trail site near the western boundary of the park. The sites typically have a fire ring and an open-air or an enclosed pit toilet. Use extreme caution with campfires and put them out completely, stirring and soaking them with water, as backcountry campsites are remote and hard to reach with firefighting equipment.

North Country Trail

The Laurentian Lakes Chapter of the North Country Trail Association cares for the campsite that is on the North Country Trail that is located 3 miles west of the parking lot on 540th Ave., north of MN–113, or 1.5 miles east of the NCT parking area on Anchor Matson Road. The NCT features another campsite 2.5 miles farther west of the park.

Firewood for Camping

If you are camping, *do not* bring your own firewood. Firewood must be purchased at the Campground Office or bought from an approved vendor in the area. This prevents the spread of the invasive emerald ash borer and other pests that threaten the park.

LODGING

Itasca State Park is blessed with the Douglas Lodge, which was dedicated in 1905 and remains one of the finest Rustic Style lodges around. The parlor retains its original look and some furnishings, and its lodge rooms are quaint. The facility has been fully modernized, but some rooms still share a bath and are sized as you might expect for the time period. There are also cabins in the Douglas Lodge and

Bear Paw areas and at Lake Ozawindib. Group lodging is available at the historic Clubhouse behind Douglas Lodge and at the Lake Ozawindib Group Center. The lodgings are all moderately priced, and two of the Douglas Lodge Itasca (Four Season) Suite units are ADA-accessible, including showers. The Douglas Lodge cabins and suites are all within a few hundred yards of the lodge and can be reserved up to a year in advance; they are typically full during summer weekends. Douglas Lodge cabins have no kitchens and are designed for those who plan to dine at Douglas Lodge or elsewhere, but the Douglas Lodge Itasca (Four Season) Suites and East Cabin have kitchenettes. Pets are *not* allowed in any Itasca lodging facilities.

Douglas Lodge Room

Douglas Lodge

The original lodge is heated and air-conditioned, and the rooms are upstairs, with no elevator. Three are suites and include a bath and shower. The four single rooms, each with a full bed and period furnishings, share 2½ bathrooms with showers down the hallway. The parlor area on the main floor has wireless Internet, and though the parlor receives some traffic from the adjacent restaurant, it remains a quiet, appealing place to read or cozy up by the fireplace. Douglas Lodge is seasonal and is open Memorial Day week-end in May through early October.

Douglas Lodge Itasca (Four Season) Suites

Set in two modern six-plexes, these one-bedroom suites sleep two to four people or up to a family of six, and include a kitchenette, AC, TV, Internet and phone. Built in a modern rustic style, they are more like what you would expect to see at a resort or condominium. Open year-round, the Douglas Lodge Itasca (Four Season) Suites are the only lodging option available in the winter.

East Cabin

Douglas Lodge Cabins

Eleven of the seasonal cabins lie north of Douglas Lodge along the ridge overlooking Lake Itasca. Cabins 5–10 were built in the Rustic Style from 1923 to 1925, and the Civilian Conservation Corps (CCC) built Cabin 12 in 1934. Cabin 11, which dates to 1911, is tucked just above the boat landing area by the Clubhouse. The cabins have one to three bedrooms, a full bath with a shower or a tub (four have ADA-accessible showers), and eight cabins have fireplaces and screen porches. They have no kitchens, refrigerators or indoor cooking facilities.

Douglas Lodge Four-plex

This seasonal log cabin also dates back to the CCC (1937–1938) era and contains studio and one-bedroom units with a fireplace, an outdoor fire ring, and a view of Lake Itasca. Although not air-conditioned, they all have screen porches and fans. Two have double beds and two have two twin beds, and the bathrooms have a tub but no shower.

East Cabin

The park has transformed the original east contact station, a CCC-era log structure from the 1930s, into a rental cabin with heating and air-conditioning, a kitchen, a fireplace, a bath and shower, and a screened gazebo. It is open seasonally and is located a short drive up the hill from Douglas Lodge.

Bear Paw Cabins

The CCC built six log cabins at Bear Paw Campground in the 1930s. The one-room, heated cabins each have a full bed and a pull-out bed, a small kitchenette, a washroom and a fireplace. Though the cabins have no tubs or showers, campground showers are available nearby.

Bear Paw Guest House

Newly renovated from the 1935 park store, this seasonal rustic guest house sleeps 10, with three bedrooms and two futon couches. It has a full kitchen, two ADA bathrooms, a fireplace, and a screened porch. This new, beautiful cabin is near the lake at the entrance to Bear Paw Campground.

Lake Ozawindib Cabin

Tucked into the northwest corner of the park, this two-bedroom seasonal cabin has two bedrooms (linens and bedding not included), a kitchenette, a living room with a fireplace, a screen porch, a dock, a canoe and a boat (no motor). There is a pit toilet but no modern bathroom or shower.

Clubhouse

Clubhouse

The two-story Clubhouse, a classic Rustic Style log structure built in 1911 and renovated in the 1980s, rents as a single unit to groups of up to 21 people. It has ten bedrooms and six bathrooms (one with an ADA-shower), a fireplace and a screen porch, but it has no indoor cooking facilities. Enjoy the wide-open living area, relax in Adirondack chairs outside, and walk the footbridge over Mary Creek to Douglas Lodge. The Clubhouse is near the excursion boat landing and the Dr. Roberts and Deer Park Trails.

Mississippi Headwaters AYH-Hostel

Mississippi Headwaters Hostel

Hostelling International's 31-bed facility is housed in the old Park Headquarters building, which dates back to 1923. The cozy log building has been updated with air-conditioning, Internet access, a laundry, a kitchen, common rooms and ADA accessibility. Located a short drive east on Forest Lane opposite the boat landing on Main Park Drive, the hostel is currently open daily from June–August and weekends in January–March, May, and September–October. The hostel sometimes closes in April, November and December, so call in advance if you're interested in staying in the hostel in those months. For more information, call (218) 266-3415 or email mhhostel@himinnesota.org.

LODGING AND CAMPING AT LA SALLE LAKE STATE RECREATION AREA (SRA)

La Salle Lake State Recreation Area (SRA) is home to a campground with 39 drive-in sites with full sewer, water and electric; 26 of the sites are reservable. The shower building has rooms with sinks, toilets and showers and there are two coin-operated washers and dryers. The campground and facilities here are likely to change and expand in the near future.

La Salle Lake State Recreation Area also currently rents two cabins located on high ground above the lake, west of the campground on Hubbard County 9. Both cabins are heated, have full kitchens and are reservable year-round.

Bert's Cabins

Although Bert's Cabins, founded by Bert and Alice Pfeifer in 1939, are not officially part of Itasca State Park, they are located on 40 acres along its northern boundary, on Wilderness Drive 1 mile west of the Headwaters. Bert and Alice's daughter, Pat, and her husband, Dave Evenwoll, now operate the resort, which is open early May through mid-October and during deer season. Pat said that Dallas and Art Savage, the original property owners, Built Cabins 1 and 6 in 1937. Cabin 4, made from balsam logs, was once the Bow and Arrow Tavern a quarter-mile down the road. When the owner failed to pay his liquor taxes and abandoned the enterprise, Bert moved the cabin to his resort. Bert's rents by the day or the week and boasts twelve modern housekeeping cabins, an outdoor playground and a swimming pool. Their website and book tell the full story of this attractive family resort, which is rooted in Itasca's history. For more information, contact: (218) 266-3312, www.bertscabins.com

Lodging Near the Park

There are numerous lodging options around Itasca and Park Rapids (20 miles south) to consider, and they range from tiny resorts with simple cabins to big, full-service resorts with a full slate of activities. The Park Rapids Chamber of Commerce (www.parkrapids.com) has a full list of lodging options in Park Rapids, and the nearby small towns of Lake George, Dorset, Nevis and Bagley also have limited lodging. Bemidji (35 miles northeast, www.visitbemidji.com) and Walker (36 miles, www.leech-lake.com) offer more distant options.

Naturalist Tour, Douglas Lodge Stairway

Park Rapids Area Community Band, Picnic Grounds

Activities at the Park

HIKING

Itasca State Park has a wide variety of trails to hike, snowshoe or ski, and these trails are available to visitors in one form or another in all seasons. The tread is friendly on all the trails, so while Itasca has no rock walls to climb or cliffs to provide distant vistas, neither does it have washed-out rivers of rock to wear out your feet. The routes leading south from Wilderness Drive are wide and grassy, and even the less-popular footpaths are generally well maintained and easy to follow. The Civilian Conservation Corps built most of the trails, and when naturalist Ben Thoma revamped them in the 1960s, his crew made them wide enough for vehicle access for fire, rescue and trail work.

The trail to the Headwaters, the first section of Dr. Roberts, and the Maadaadizi Trail are level, wide and accessible. Most trails have some changes in elevation as they traverse the glacial hills, and a vigorous hike will provide at least a moderate workout. Depending on the length of the route chosen, one could end up on a loop of 8 miles or more, traveling through remote areas of the park with few other hikers. That adds a strenuous component to the trip, especially under adverse conditions.

As you go along, allow time to appreciate the sights, sounds and smells of the forests, lakes and wetlands. Itasca is short on mountain vistas but rich in smaller treasures like wildflowers and birds, so take time to look down and see what's going on at your feet, and look up to see what's happening in the trees. The bog areas, such as those on Dr. Roberts Trail, hold good examples of tiny plants, including many species that you probably have never seen before. The numbered stakes and booklet for that trail will help you identify some of them.

Hiking Considerations

Trail distances in this guide are based on my GPS, and reflect side trips to lakes and other points of interest that most people will also take, so they may exceed official distances by 10–15 percent. The hiking times listed are based on a 1.5 mph average overall pace, including stops, so the times listed will vary greatly from person to person and are intended only as a general guideline.

The North Country Trail has four segments within Itasca State Park, and to prevent confusion for through-hikers, the guide goes from east to west on all of them. Hikers going from west to east on any NCT segment will need to reverse these directions.

Poison Ivy

Trail Safety

As you travel down the trails, you will find inviting detours to lakeshores, streams, berry patches, wetlands, and scenic overlooks. Stopping at these locations is just fine; otherwise, it's a great idea to stay on the marked trail to minimize the impact on the natural beauty around the trail edges, which are often rich in wildflowers. Given the surroundings, it is also easy to quickly get lost and start walking in circles, especially if you are unaccustomed to navigating in the woods. The same applies to some historic but unmarked CCC and forestry trails, which are no longer maintained. They may begin with a clear footpath, but disappear in a winding labyrinth of deer trails. You are also much more likely to be exposed to ticks and poison ivy in the deep grass or brush away from the cleared path.

WEATHER
Temperatures can plummet as darkness falls on the short days of winter, so winter travel requires an extra measure of caution and planning. Whether you are skiing or walking, be sure to carefully gauge your abilities and seasonal weather conditions so that you can return safely. Whatever the season, bring adequate water with you on anything but a short hike, as any water along the trail requires purification.

Trail Essentials
- Proper clothing and footwear (especially in winter or adverse weather)
- Water
- Matches
- Sunscreen
- Trail map and compass
- Insect repellent (spring, summer, fall)

Hiking and Passport Clubs
The Minnesota State Parks Hiking Club consists of one trail from each Minnesota State Park, with patch awards for those who hike 25 or more miles of designated trails. Itasca's designated trail loop begins at Douglas Lodge and heads south 1.5 miles on Ozawindib Trail. From there, turn west on the Crossover Trail for 0.7 mile to Deer Park Trail. Go north on Deer Park Trail for 1.5 miles to return to Douglas Lodge.

Passport Club members get rewards for visiting many or all of the state parks. Kits, currently $14.95 each, are available in the gift shop or by ordering from DNR Information Center in St. Paul, (888) 646-6367.

NATURALIST PROGRAMS

Itasca is renowned for its naturalist programs, which are held year-round, with a full schedule in the summer and early fall. Programs vary from Circle Time Under the Pines, a 45-minute program for young children, to the GPS Challenge, Music Under the Pines, Archery in the Park, and Dr. Roberts Plant Identification Walk. History is a popular theme, especially the walks highlighting the Civilian Conservation Corps and the Old Timer's Cabin, the Pioneer Cemetery Walk and the Headwaters History Hike. The park naturalists and summer Naturalist Corps workers have developed interpretive trail signage and the popular educational displays in the Jacob V. Brower Visitor Center. They are the heart of the park, bringing the Itasca story to life through a variety of means to visitors with all levels of interest.

Bike Trail

BIKING

Bicycles are rolling everywhere on a typical summer day in Itasca State Park, as visitors enjoy the paved trail that runs all the way from Douglas Lodge to the Headwaters. Many continue on Wilderness Drive, sharing the road with auto traffic, to complete a 16-mile loop around the park. Miles of bike routes run through the surrounding area, both on paved trails and on highways, making Itasca a haven for bicyclists.

Bike Trail

Beginning at Douglas Lodge, the bike trail climbs hills and past big pines, crossing the road by the East Entrance station at Brower Visitor Center. From there, the trail continues up and down moderate hills, passing near Preacher's

Grove and Peace Pipe Vista. The trail has two-way bike traffic, so be sure to keep to the right, especially around blind corners and on the hills. Construction begun in 2013 widened the trail from 8 feet to 10 feet and revised a few trouble spots between the Jacob V. Brower Visitor Center and the descent to Bear Paw Campground. A redesigned trail stays along the north side of Main Park Drive to the Boat Harbor. From there, the trail to the Headwaters will be rebuilt along the existing route. The redesigned trail stays along the north side of Main Park Drive to the Boat Harbor, where it crosses Main Park Drive and runs to the Headwaters along the east side of Lake Itasca along the old route.

Wilderness Drive

Wilderness Drive

Wilderness Drive brings you west from the Headwaters and Mary Gibbs Mississippi Headwaters Center along a paved road that was once a rough gravel trail. The drive goes straight west until it reaches the road to Lake Ozawindib, where it turns south and soon narrows into a one-way road. Paved in 2012, the surface is smooth and makes for a pleasant drive or vigorous bike ride, as the hills get steeper and the curves get tighter south of Bohall Trail. Wilderness Drive brings you to several hiking trails along the way. The road turns east at Two Spot Trail, crosses Nicollet Creek and passes by Elk Lake and provides access to Nicollet, DeSoto, and Aiton Heights Fire Tower Trails. It also crosses Deer Park and Ozawindib Trails. At Mary Lake boat landing, it widens to a two-lane road and returns to Douglas Lodge or Brower Visitor Center.

Ozawindib Bike Trail

This paved trail, in the planning stage in 2016, will begin at the Headwaters and travel west, connecting with Wilderness Drive at the beginning of the one-way segment near Lake Ozawindib Group Center.

Itasca Sports, Boat Landing

Directions for Biking to the Park

Currently those biking into the park can enter via the South, East or North Entrance roads and connect to the designated bike trail from there. A separate bike trail entering near the East Entrance is a future possibility. The span of Main Park Drive that leads from the Jacob V. Brower Visitor Center to the Headwaters carries the vast majority of auto traffic, but can be ridden with caution by experienced road bikers. Others should use the designated bike trail. Bike rentals are available at Itasca Sports (at the boat landing) and at Northern Cycle in Park Rapids.

Hazards

Roads and trails are slippery when wet, and it goes without saying that bikers use roadways at their own risk and should always wear a helmet. The paved Bike Trail, newly redesigned in 2014, still has two-way traffic. It has fewer tight corners than the old route but still has some hills and turns. Observe the 15 mph speed limit in these areas. Backroads and woods can be buggy in the summer, and although it's easy to outrun mosquitoes, deer flies may exceed 15 mph. (A dryer sheet partially tucked under your helmet can be helpful when repellent alone won't do the job.) If you travel on US-71 use extra caution, ride single file, and wear high-visibility clothing, due to the high volume of traffic and deeply cut rumble strips at the highway's edge.

Headwaters 100 Bike Ride

Sponsored annually by Itascatur Ski, Bike, and Run Club, usually on the fourth Saturday of September, this popular ride offers 100-, 75- and 42-mile rides around area roads, finishing on the Heartland Trail into Park Rapids. The two longer rides travel around Wilderness Drive in Itasca State Park. Visit www. itascatur.org/bike.shtml for details.

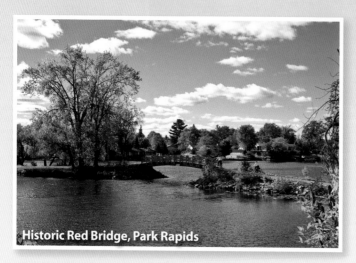
Historic Red Bridge, Park Rapids

BIKE TRAILS NEAR THE PARK
Heartland State Trail

First developed in 1976, the Heartland Trail was one of the first rail-to-trail projects in the country. The current trail, beginning near downtown Park Rapids, runs through Heartland Park on a level, paved surface all the way to Cass Lake. The restaurants and shops in Dorset and Nevis are especially popular with riders, and Akeley has a park with a Paul Bunyan statue. Park Rapids and Walker offer a full lineup of dining and shopping choices. Inline skaters should be on the lookout for dips and bumps due to roots, which are especially prevalent in stands of aspen and balsam poplar. The 27-mile stretch to Walker has a parallel grassy trail for snowmobiles and horses.

The landscape is highly varied, with hardwoods, especially oak, and aspen, jack pine and red pine lining much of the route. There are also open fields, farms, wetlands and lakes along the way. Wildflowers, prominent and varying with the seasons, are often different from those in the surrounding woodlands, with more prairie plants, such as leadplant, rough blazing star, and purple prairie clover, represented on this old railroad grade. Birds and mammals common to

Itasca State Park are also abundant along this trail, which is especially loaded with squirrels and white-tailed deer. Long-term planning is underway to build a bicycle trail connecting Itasca State Park to the Heartland Trail near Park Rapids.

Paul Bunyan State Trail

This 120-mile trail connects Crow Wing State Park, near Brainerd, to Walker, Bemidji and Lake Bemidji State Park. Like the Heartland Trail, it is a mostly level, easily accessible trail running on an old railroad grade. One scenic section, between Hackensack and MN-34 near Akeley, has 9 miles of curves and hills through the forest with grades of up to 8 percent. Riders who want a less challenging route should take the Shin-Go-Be Connection Trail, which runs north along MN-371 to Walker.

Another route to Bemidji, the Mississippi River Trail route, links existing roadways and bike trails and runs from Itasca along the entire Mississippi River. Beginning north on Clearwater County 2 from the north entrance of Itasca, it turns right on Clearwater County 40 (230th Street), which becomes Hubbard County 9 and continues past La Salle Lake State Recreation Area. For more information, visit: http://www.dot.state.mn.us/bike/mrt/

Hernando DeSoto Lake

Water Sports

"The movement of a canoe is like a reed in the wind. Silence is part of it, and the sounds of lapping water, bird songs, and wind in the trees."
—Sigurd Olson, *The Singing Wilderness*

CANOEING AND KAYAKING

Climb into a canoe and paddle around one of the 100 lakes in Itasca State Park and you will experience the joy that Sigurd Olson has shared in his books praising the north country of Minnesota. Fittingly, Lake Itasca is the park's largest lake, and at 1,065 acres, its length and shape provide long stretches of sheltered shoreline, which allow for good paddling even in moderate wind. Elk, Mary and Ozawindib Lakes have boat landings, so they are also good choices for canoeing or kayaking. Several other smaller lakes are reachable from roads, though boat landings are not generally developed, and most interior lakes require a portage of 0.5 mile or more. Itasca Sports rents canoes and kayaks, just for use on Lake Itasca, at the Boat Landing on Main Park Drive, and there are also rowboats for rent on Mary Lake, Lake Ozawindib and Elk Lake.

THE MISSISSIPPI RIVER WATER TRAIL

The Mississippi River Water Trail begins at the park, and you can access it from the Headwaters area, from Gulsvig Landing off MN-200, or at multiple points beyond. The 62 river miles to Bemidji are designated "wild and scenic" and live up to the name, and there are rest stops and campsites along the way. The first 5 miles, up to Wanagan Landing, are gentle and winding but go through a shallow, wide marshy area where it can be difficult to follow the main channel. The river merges with Sucker Brook, a trout stream which flows through the spruce-and-tamarack forest of Iron Springs Bog Scientific and Natural Area. From Wanagan Landing to Clearwater County 2 you portage over Vekin's Dam into a narrow valley, where there are Class I rapids and sand bars to negotiate. Beyond LaSalle Creek and Coffee Pot Landing, the Mississippi winds through a series of shallow wetlands, some of which extend for 5 miles. These can be very buggy and confusing to navigate, especially after midsummer or in low water. If the gauge at Coffee Pot Landing reads less than 1.9 feet, paddling beyond that point will be difficult. For current water levels, visit: http://www.dnr.state.mn.us/river_levels/index.html

For detailed information, be sure to get the DNR's Mississippi River Water Trail Guide, which is available at the Jacob V. Brower Visitor Center or online. It has excellent descriptions of the sights and lists the river conditions. You can download it here: http://www.dnr.state.mn.us/watertrails/mississippiriver/one.html

Lake Itasca Swimming Beach

SWIMMING

Is there a better place to be on a hot summer day than the swimming beach at Itasca State Park? With its 1940s log changing house, picnic tables, sand beach, volleyball court and clean water, it has always been one of the most popular places in the park. There are no lifeguards, so be sure to constantly supervise children and inexperienced swimmers.

BOATING AND FISHING

Lake Itasca is the largest and busiest fishing spot in the park, with a double boat ramp, a big parking lot, and, like all lakes in the park, a 10 mph speed limit. Paddleboats, fishing boats, pontoons and motors for use on Lake Itasca are available at Itasca Sports Rental, which is open May–October. You must have a life jacket on board and readily accessible for each occupant of a boat or canoe, and actually wearing it is a great idea, especially when the water is cold. The large lakes within the park have special fishing regulations. Boat landings are also located on Mary, Ozawindib and Elk Lakes within Itasca State Park and LaSalle Lake in the nearby La Salle Lake State Recreation Area (see page 52).

There is also a fishing pier on the south end of the East Arm of Lake Itasca, below Douglas Lodge, near the Coborn's Lake Itasca Cruises boat dock. A fishing pier is also planned for the boat landing on Lake Ozawindib; it will be built by the Friends of Itasca group.

There can be good fishing in lakes throughout the area, including those within the park. Nonresidents who intend to fish in the park will need a fishing license; Minnesota residents can currently fish without a license in lakes that are totally contained within state park property, although this could change in the future. This does not include state recreation areas or areas that require a trout stamp.

Walleye opener in early May is a huge holiday in northern Minnesota, drawing crowds to lakes everywhere. Bass season typically begins around Memorial Day, with muskie season around the first of June.

Lake Itasca is by far the most popular for all species, and walleye opener can be a bit of a mob scene. Most of the other small lakes scattered throughout the park have a mix of panfish, including pumpkinseed sunfish, bluegills, and the smaller green sunfish, which can be the primary species on some lakes. Some of the small, deep lakes sheltered in the valley on South Entrance Road south of

Mary Lake have so little wind to turn the water over and bring oxygen to the depths that they support few or no fish.

AQUATIC INVASIVE SPECIES

In a real respect, Minnesota's lakes—including all of Itasca's—are threatened by aquatic invasive species. Itasca's lakes, though free of significant problems as of 2013, are vulnerable to the same invasives that have infested other northern Minnesota lakes, threatening the local ecosystem, harming gamefish, and making it harder to enjoy the great outdoors. Help keep invasive pests like zebra mussels and Eurasian milfoil out of Itasca's pristine lakes and streams by following the DNR's guidelines for reducing this risk! Drain it, clean it and dry it! See the DNR's webpage for details: http://www.dnr.state.mn.us/invasives/index_aquatic.html

North Country Trail

Winter Sports in Itasca

Itasca State Park is still a great place to come in winter months, despite the cold and snow that accompany a trip in this season. The Headwaters of the

Mississippi take on a special charm when snow forms pillows on the rocks, and the park's trails are as beautiful for skiing and snowmobiling as they are for hiking.

FACILITIES

The Jacob V. Brower Visitor Center is open variable hours during winter, although the front lobby, with restrooms and water available, may have extended hours. Other facilities, including Douglas Lodge, Forest Inn and the Mary Gibbs Mississippi Headwaters Center at the Headwaters are typically closed in winter. Ski licenses (required on all public and park trails), vehicle passes and maps for Itasca's skiing, snowmobiling and winter trails are available at the Visitor Center.

LODGING AND CAMPING

One loop of Pine Ridge Campground is kept open for winter camping. Bear Paw Campground and the group camps are closed, and shower buildings are only open through mid-October. To reach the winter camping loop, turn on Main Park Drive opposite the Lake Itasca boat landing. Backcountry camping is also possible in the winter.

Mississippi Headwaters Hostel, located on the winter campground road in the Old Park Headquarters Building, is open weekends January–March and weekends in May. The hostel is closed in November, December and April. For information, contact: (218) 266-3415, http://www.hiusa.org/parkrapids

Douglas Lodge's Itasca (Four Season) Suites are open year-round. The two six-plex buildings are located near Douglas Lodge and house modern two-room suites that can accommodate 1–4 adults or a family of 4–6. They include a full bath and kitchen. Contact: (866) 857-2757.

Winter lodging and camping information at the park is liable to change, so be sure to check for current information at any of these facilities. If park lodging is full or unavailable, lodging is available year-round in the Park Rapids, Walker, Bagley and Bemidji areas.

North Country Trail

SNOWSHOEING

On a nice winter weekend, trails will be busy with the shuffling of snowshoes. The Jacob V. Brower Visitor Center has them available to rent, both in the traditional rawhide mesh and new rubber/aluminum varieties. The most popular snowshoeing trails are the Dr. Roberts, Brower, Schoolcraft and Headwaters Trails. Maadaadizi Trail, right at the visitor center, is available for a short trip. The Mary Lake Trail, from Forest Inn to the Mary Lake boat landing, and LaSalle Trail, by Pine Ridge Campground, are also open to snowshoeing, as is any trail not groomed for skiing. Alaskan snowshoes (or similar large varieties) are best if the snow is deep and unpacked, but the smaller lightweight varieties work fine once someone has broken a trail. Hiking or snowshoeing on ski trails is not recommended, but if you do need to walk, please stay to the edge of the trail and avoid walking on classic ski tracks or in the middle of the skate ski lane.

Snowmobiling near Park Rapids

SNOWMOBILING

Itasca State Park, with its beautiful scenery and 32 miles of groomed trails within the park, is the hub for area snowmobile enthusiasts. Like spokes on a wheel, the Itasca trails reach out to trail systems in the surrounding communities of Park Rapids, Nevis, Bemidji, Bagley, Mahnomen and Detroit Lakes. The Forest Riders club from Park Rapids currently grooms the Itasca loop and has placed directional signs throughout their trail system, as have many other clubs in the area. Each sign is numbered, mapped, gives distances and directional arrows to nearby points, and has a GPS coordinate (UTM notation). The trail around Itasca is Route 23. A current snowmobile map, available in the Jacob V. Brower Visitor Center and at area businesses, is essential to navigate the continually evolving maze of hundreds of miles of groomed trails in the area. For more information, contact the Park Rapids Chamber of Commerce at (218) 732-4111, www. parkrapids.com, or the snowmobile clubs in your preferred direction of travel.

ICE FISHING

Lake Itasca and Mary Lake are the easiest lakes to access for ice fishing, although all the lakes in the park are open. Many of the lakes have special regulations, so check with the park staff and read the Minnesota fishing regulations before venturing out. If you are unfamiliar with "hard water" fishing, local bait and tackle shops can help you get started. If you're new to ice fishing, you should know that it is never 100 percent safe to walk or drive on the ice, especially in unpredictable areas around inlets, outlets, springs or any moving water. At least 4" of new, clear, solid ice is needed to walk, and 8–12" for a car, more for a truck. Be aware that ice that has been snow-covered or "rotten" late-season ice during the spring melt are notoriously weak and dangerous for travel. When in doubt, stay off! For more information, visit: http://www.dnr.state.mn.us/safety/ice/index.html

Deer Park Trail

SKIING

Cross-country skiing is one of the park's main winter attractions, although several inches of snow are required to build up a good base under the big pines. Itasca maintains 28 miles of groomed trails for all ability levels.

Snow depth and trail conditions are updated regularly on the Itasca State Park website and can be obtained by visiting or calling the Jacob V. Brower Visitor Center. Reports for Itasca, Park Rapids, Bemidji and other area trails also show up on www.skinnyski.com. Of course, skiing options can change from year to year. For an in-depth look at the skiing options in Itasca State Park, see the special section on page 139.

A Minnesota Ski Pass is required on all Itasca, Soaring Eagle and Bemidji trails, and passes are available for purchase at the Visitor Center, online, or wherever fishing and hunting licenses are sold.

Nearby Ski Trails:

There are a variety of ski trails near the park, as well. These include:

- Soaring Eagle Trail: This 10-kilometer complex of skate/classic trails for all levels is located on US-71 about 11 miles south of Itasca State Park, or 8.5 miles north of Park Rapids. The trails are regularly groomed by Itascatur Club, and they have a warming chalet. For more information, visit: www.itascatur.org

- Maplelag: With 64 kilometers of ski and mountain bike trails, this cozy destination resort is an hour away, located 20 miles northeast of Detroit Lakes, MN. Their manicured trails are usually the first in the area to be skiable, and day passes are available. This would be a good place to stay and take a day trip to Itasca, though once you get settled in here, you may not wish to leave. Contact: www.maplelag.com

- Rainbow Resort: Located 4 miles south of MN-113 on County 35, Rainbow has 23 kilometers of groomed trails as well as cabin rentals. They will also usually have snow and groomed trails before Itasca. Contact: www.rainbowresort.com
- Bemidji: The area has several trails, including the lighted Montebello Trail in town. For more information: www.visitbemidji.com
- Walker-Hackensack: Lake Country Nordic Ski Club maintains mostly classic trails in Cass County, most are an hour from Itasca. Shingobee has advanced classic/skating on MN-34 near Akeley. For more information: http://www.co.cass.mn.us/maps/map_trails.html

SKIJORING

Feeling bored with the routine of cross-country skiing? Do you have a larger dog that loves to run? If you answered yes to both questions, then you should try skijoring, the art of skiing with a dog. Skijoring is fulfilling for both of you and sure to put a smile on your face. In addition to skis and poles (skate or classic), you will need a skijoring or dog sled harness that fits your dog, a waist harness for you, and a rope with an elastic section to cushion the pull. Get some advice from an experienced skijorer before you go out there, and provide hydration and snacks for you and your dog, as it is a lot of work for both parties. The west side of Wilderness Drive to Nicollet Trail and Two Spot Trail are groomed for skijoring and skate skiing.

ATV/OHM TRAILS

There are no designated trails in Itasca State Park or La Salle Lake SRA for off-highway vehicles, but there are hundreds of miles of forest trails in the area that are open to ATVs (Forest Riders and Round River Drive Trails), Off-Highway Motorcycles (Martineau Trail), or both (Schoolcraft ATV Trail). Contact the Forest Riders or check the parkrapids.com website for the latest local information or contact Minnesota State Parks and Trails for statewide information.

Showy Lady's Slippers, Brower Trail

Visiting Itasca with Children—and Pets!

Although children will never lose their sense of joy in the discovery of nature, they may lack the opportunity to see the natural world firsthand. Even in smaller rural cities children may see gardens and lawns as the only representatives of the natural world for much of their lives. Itasca offers a rich opportunity to expose young people to the joys and challenges of the outdoors. Here are some suggestions for kids of all ages.

- The Jacob V. Brower Visitor Center is a great place to start. Inside you will find displays of plants, animals and birds that you might see at the park, depictions of early Indian life, stories of discovery of the park, and an interactive three-dimensional map of Itasca State Park. There are also videos to watch.

- Try out a few of the short hiking trails, especially with young children. The Maadaadizi Trail is a half-mile, level trail with interpretive signs and begins at the Brower Visitor Center.

- Dr. Roberts Trail begins on the lakefront below Douglas Lodge. The two-mile trail has numbered signs with a booklet that is a key to identifying the plants along the trail. The first 0.3 mile is an especially easy hike to the Old Timer's Cabin. Bring a small digital camera so children can take pictures; this really helps to focus their attention and engage them with the subject.

- Naturalist programs are scheduled many days a week in the summer season and target all ages. With a focus on learning through stories, crafts, songs and outdoor activities, "Circle Time Under the Pines" is a great one-hour intro to nature topics for ages 2–5. Activities, usually requiring adult accompaniment, are listed on the Itasca State Park event calendar online or in the visitor centers.

- The Junior Park Naturalist program through the Minnesota DNR provides educators, group leaders and homeschoolers with three 28-page activity booklets about Pinelands, Hardwoods and Prairie, and a certificate upon completion of each. There is also a Park Explorer series and the Project Learning Tree, a collection of family activities designed for use at home or at the park. (For more information, look under kids' programs or activities on the DNR State Park website.)

- The Headwaters is also a required stop, and kids and parents alike will enjoy the challenge of crossing the Mississippi on the rocks. Most end up in the water sooner or later and wade in the clear stream that leaves Lake Itasca on its way to New Orleans.

- The waterfront—especially the beach—is a kid magnet in the summer, especially on a warm, sunny day. The water is usually warm enough to swim by mid-June, depending on the year, and can stay warm until Labor Day. Supervision of swimmers is necessary, as lifeguards are not available. Keep a close eye on toddlers and young children, as there are no securely fenced play areas here.

- Kids typically enjoy fishing; your best bet to keep them interested is to find a spot with a lot of panfish or perch, regardless of size. Flatten the barb of the hook with pliers to make catch-and-release easier. If you don't plan on bringing your own watercraft, Itasca Sports (located at the boat landing) has boats, motors, canoes, kayaks, pontoons, fishing gear and bikes to rent.

- Biking along the trail from the Headwaters to the Jacob V. Brower Visitor Center is one of the most popular activities at Itasca. Wear a helmet, stay on the right half of the trail, and observe the speed limit of 15 mph, as there are some sharp corners and hills along the way. The north part of the current bike trail, which connects the Brower Center, both campgrounds, and lakeside attractions to the Headwaters, was recently redesigned and rerouted.

VISITING ITASCA WITH PETS

Dogs are welcome on the trails and in campgrounds, but they must be quiet, well behaved and be on no more than a six-foot leash or crated at all times. Only service animals are typically allowed in state park buildings, lodging or cabins. Quality pet care facilities and dog-friendly hotels (www.dogfriendly.com) are available in Park Rapids and Bemidji.

Nearby Attractions

For details on any of these attractions, retail opportunities and events, contact the respective Chamber of Commerce, as details, dates and even businesses may change or come and go from year to year.

GAS, FOOD, SHOPPING AND LODGING

Itasca State Park Area:

Gas and convenience stores, each with a lunch counter, are located at the Rock Creek Store at the North Entrance on County 122, Itasca Junction just east of the East Entrance on MN-200/US-71, Lake George at the Woodland Store, 8 miles east on MN-200, and Emmaville Store, 10 miles south of Lake George on County 4. Lobo's Bar and Grill, located on MN-200 between the North and East Entrances, also has cabins for rent.

Park Rapids (20 miles south on US-71):

It should come as no surprise that Park Rapids hosted the Governor's Fishing Opener in 2013. Not only is it the epicenter of fishing and outdoor recreation in the region, it has the full range of shopping, dining, lodging and services that a visitor would look for.

Dorset (20 miles south on US-71 to Park Rapids, then 5 miles east on MN-34, then 1.5 miles north on MN-226):

The "Restaurant Capital of the World" is home to some locally famous dining options, including everything from Mexican and Italian food to traditional dining. "Taste of Dorset" occurs on the first Sunday in August and packs the tiny town with hungry people looking for street food, games and fun. Dorset also has a B&B and shops offering books, gifts, photos and clothing.

Emmaville (8 miles east on MN-200/US-71, then 10 miles south on County 4):

The Emmaville Store, located in "The Biggest Little Town in the World," is a gas station, convenience store, café, a small motel and cabin, and campground all rolled into one.

Bemidji (14 miles east on US-71/MN-200 and 16 miles north on US-71):

Bemidji, a regional hub for shopping, services and transportation, has Bemidji Regional Airport, with connections to Minneapolis. A full range of hotels, motels, resorts, recreation, camping and dining is available.

Bagley (28 miles north on MN-200 and MN-92:

Bagley is known as the "Gateway to Itasca," thanks to its historic connections to the early days of Itasca State Park. It has groceries, gas, a bakery, a motel, restaurants, a hardware store and other shops. Visit www.bagleymn.us for more information.

LaSalle Lake

La Salle Lake State Recreation Area (SRA) and Scientific Natural Area (SNA)

This 986-acre gem, added to Minnesota's state park and recreation system in 2011, includes 238-acre LaSalle Lake, Minnesota's second deepest at 213 feet. The SRA is located on Hubbard County 9, 4.5 miles west of Becida and about 10 miles north of Itasca State Park, which administers camping and lodging within the SRA. With camping, hiking, snowshoeing, hunting and fishing in season, the SRA offers new opportunities for local residents and visitors, while it protects one of the most pristine lakes in the state. The surroundings, a mixed hardwood and pine forest, abound with wildflowers and birds.

CULTURAL AND NATURAL HISTORY

LaSalle valley is rich in cultural as well as natural history, and humans have lived there for thousands of years. Recent archaeological excavations near LaSalle Creek unearthed evidence of Brainerd Ware ceramics, dating back to 3,180 years ago, from the Early Woodland Indian Elk Lake Culture.

LASALLE CREEK

From its source in the northeast corner of Itasca State Park, LaSalle Creek runs north through a deep glacial tunnel valley, passing through Big LaSalle Lake and the tiny sliver of Middle LaSalle Lake. From

Mississippi River, La Salle Lake SNA River Overlook Trail

there it winds north through wetlands, entering the south end of LaSalle Lake, site of the SRA. After flowing north from LaSalle Lake, LaSalle Creek runs under Hubbard County 9, through an old logging sluice and dam and the 268-acre SNA, finally entering the Mississippi River, which borders the SNA to the west.

La Salle Lake SNA protects a small part of the Mississippi Valley landscape, including upland pine and hardwood forests, tamarack and spruce wetlands, and an old-growth white cedar swamp. A mature jack pine forest, which once covered high ground leading to a view of the confluence of LaSalle Creek and the Mississippi River, was hit hard by a severe storm on July 3, 2012, nearly wiping out the stand. Only a few hardy remnants remain after salvage logging of damaged and downed trees, rarely done in an SNA, was carried out to minimize fire danger and pest infestations, such as jack pine budworm. The ground was scarified (artificially disturbed) to encourage natural reproduction and sprouting of the jack pine seeds left behind. Fallen trees impede travel off the beaten path in the mature red and white pine forest east of LaSalle Creek, which also sustained heavy damage, although the white cedars remain mostly intact. The SNA and surrounding area continue to provide rich habitat for wolves, river otters and other mammals, and a host of birds from eagles and ospreys to woodland warblers. The only trail in the SNA is a 0.75-mile path,

River Overlook Trail, which goes through the heart of the blowdown area, but it still provides a nice view at the point overlooking the confluence of LaSalle Creek and the Mississippi River.

Black Bear Guest House

RECREATION OPPORTUNITIES IN THE SRA

Camping is available at 39 sites. The are 26 reservable sites; call (866) 857-2757 to make reservations. All sites have full sewer, water and electric hookups. There is a campground building with showers and modern bathrooms. The Black Bear Guest House, with a beautiful view overlooking LaSalle Lake, sleeps 10 in three bedrooms and a futon. It has a bath with a shower, a full kitchen, a deck, and a picnic area with a fire ring and a gas grill. The two-bedroom Lone Wolf Cabin is uphill from the lake and sleeps four, with similar, but smaller, amenities. The cabins include blankets, comforters and pillows, but no linens, and are open April–November. Access to the cabins is via the Boat Landing entrance.

Swimming is possible at the small beach near the boat landing below the campground, though the water in this deep lake tends to be cool throughout the summer, and the bottom drops steeply down to 50' in this corner of the lake.

A snowmobile trail enters the campground from county forest lands to the east and exits via the campground entrance to the trail along Hubbard County 9. A North Country Snowmobile Club trail (Bemidji) along the western SRA boundary connects to other regional trails.

PICNIC AREA

The west entrance to the SRA now has a beautiful picnic area with a shelter, restrooms, a boardwalk to a fishing pier, and a carry-down canoe landing on LaSalle Creek. Note that the drive-in boat ramp is separate, at the Boat Landing entrance.

Challenge Trail, La Salle Lake SRA

CANOEING, KAYAKING, FISHING AND HUNTING IN THE SRA

Canoeing or kayaking on LaSalle Lake is ideal. Unless gusts are sweeping down the length of the lake, the high hills around the lake, reaching nearly 200' above lake level in places, protect the lake from summer winds. You can also reach the Mississippi River by paddling down LaSalle Creek north of the road, though it is subject to windfalls. The small boat landing has limited parking and a basic boat ramp, and there is a carry-down canoe landing in the Picnic Area. All lakes in Itasca State Park and La Salle Lake State Recreation Area have speed limit restrictions (typically 10 mph), but check for current information with the Jacob V. Brower Visitor Center at (218) 699-7251 if there are no signs at the landing.

Fishing on LaSalle Lake can be good, but the fish limits are lower, due to the small area of productive water (littoral zone) around the edge of the lake, which limits the sustainable fish population. The limits as of 2015 are: two walleyes, five crappies, five sunfish, ten perch, and bass catch-and-release only. This could change in the future. The steep contours of the lake could provide shore fishing opportunities for those without a boat.

Hunting is allowed in the SRA and on adjacent public lands in season, but keep current with hunting and trapping regulations, which can vary greatly from year to year. There is no hunting in the campground/day-use zone in the northeast quarter of the recreation area, extending across LaSalle Creek.

Arco Lake

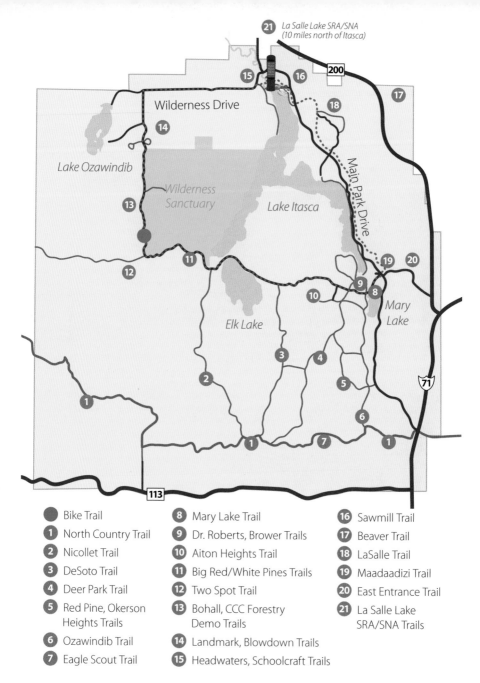

21 La Salle Lake SRA/SNA
(10 miles north of Itasca)

200

17

Wilderness Drive

15 16 18

14

Lake Ozawindib

Main Park Drive

13 Wilderness Sanctuary

Lake Itasca

11

12

19 20

9 8

10 Mary Lake

Elk Lake

3 4

2 5 71

1 6

1 7 1

113

- ● **Bike Trail**
- **1** North Country Trail
- **2** Nicollet Trail
- **3** DeSoto Trail
- **4** Deer Park Trail
- **5** Red Pine, Okerson Heights Trails
- **6** Ozawindib Trail
- **7** Eagle Scout Trail
- **8** Mary Lake Trail
- **9** Dr. Roberts, Brower Trails
- **10** Aiton Heights Trail
- **11** Big Red/White Pines Trails
- **12** Two Spot Trail
- **13** Bohall, CCC Forestry Demo Trails
- **14** Landmark, Blowdown Trails
- **15** Headwaters, Schoolcraft Trails
- **16** Sawmill Trail
- **17** Beaver Trail
- **18** LaSalle Trail
- **19** Maadaadizi Trail
- **20** East Entrance Trail
- **21** La Salle Lake SRA/SNA Trails

Itasca State Park's visitor centers and website have free summer and winter trail maps, which are regularly updated with changes to the trail system. La Salle Lake SRA trails are new and liable to change, so be sure to obtain a current map for that area.

Hiking in Itasca

From Itasca State Park's first years, its trails have been constantly changing. Here is a detailed guide to the park's hiking trails for all four seasons.

Itasca's trail names tell the story of the park. The trail narratives here cover the history of each trail and its name, as well as the features and attractions that make each trail special. (Note: The GPS coordinates listed in this book are expressed in the degrees, minutes, decimal notation.) When hiking, please note that wildflowers along the trail are protected and should never be picked or removed.

DeSoto Trail

Trail Basics

Aiton Heights Trail and Fire Tower

Beaver Trail

Blowdown Trail

Bohall Trail

CCC Forestry Demonstration Area

Deer Park Trail

Hiking Trails

Note the trail name, distance and hiking difficulty. Then turn to the page number for the specific trail guide.

● = easy
○ = moderate
● = strenuous

Big White Pine Trail and Big Red Pine/Bison Kill Site Trail

Brower Trail

DeSoto Trail

Dr. Roberts Trail

East Entrance CCC Section Corner Trail

Landmark Interpretive Trail

LaSalle Trail

Mary Lake Trail and Deer Exclosure

Eagle Scout Trail/North Country Trail

North Country Trail
DeSoto Trail and Morrison Trail

Hiking nearby on the North Country Trail

Headwaters Trail

Maadaadizi Trail

Nicollet Trail

North Country Trail
Morrison Trail to the Park's
West Boundary

HIKING GUIDE

NCT South Entrance to Ozawindib

Ozawindib Trail

Red Pine Trail

Sawmill Trail

SAWMILL HILL
IN MEMORY OF
ROY HEMMERICH
WHO OWNED & OPERATED THE
SAWMILL ON THIS SITE FROM
1952 - 1972

Two Spot Trail

La Salle Lake SRA Campground Trail

La Salle Lake SRA/SNA River
Overlook Trail

Okerson Heights Trail

Schoolcraft Trail

La Salle Lake SRA Challenge Trail

○ **North Country Trail—South Entrance Road to Ozawindib Trail**
1.2 miles one-way; pg. 115

○ **Ozawindib Trail**
2.8 miles one-way; pg. 117

○ **Okerson Heights Trail**
0.5 mile one-way; pg. 119

○ **Red Pine Trail**
1.3 miles one-way; pg. 121

● **Sawmill Trail**
0.6 mile one-way; pg. 123

● **Schoolcraft Trail**
1.1 miles one-way, pg. 124

○ **Two Spot Trail**
2.2 miles one-way; pg. 126

LA SALLE LAKE SRA AND SNA HIKING TRAILS

○ **La Salle Lake SRA Campground Trail**
1.2 miles one-way; pg. 128

● **La Salle Lake SRA Challenge Trail**
7.2-mile loop; pg. 130

● **La Salle Lake SRA/SNA River Overlook Trail**
1.1 mile one-way; pg. 133

Aiton Heights Trail and Fire Tower

Aiton Heights Trail

The Aiton Heights Trail actually begins on Ozawindib Trail just south of Wilderness Drive and crosses Deer Park Trail on its way to the fire tower. Many visitors who are just going to the tower park in the parking lot on Wilderness Drive and take the short walk from there. The tower is closed in inclement weather and during winter.

Distance/Time: 1 mile round-trip from the tower parking lot (1 hour) or 3 miles round-trip from Douglas Lodge (2-plus hours)

Difficulty: Moderate

Special Attractions: Panoramic view from the 100' tower

Hazards: Use caution and monitor children on the tower

Winter: The busy connecting trail from Ozawindib to Deer Park is groomed for classic skiers

Facilities: Parking area and toilet

Trailhead: The trail begins on Ozawindib Trail, although many visitors begin at the parking lot off Wilderness Drive

GPS at Trailhead: (Beginning on Ozawindib Trail, 0.5 mile south of Douglas Lodge): N 47° 11.026' W 095° 10.269'

TRAIL HISTORY. Aiton Heights was named for Prof. George B. Aiton, who made botanical observations in the park in 1891. The CCC built the 100' tower at the Forestry School and reconstructed it at its current location in 1937–1940. Since its fire-spotting days ended in the 1950s, it has become more valuable for education and public relations. Olaf Qualley, a seasonal forestry employee for many years, was well known for presenting talks on forestry and then handing out "Ancient and Honorable Order of Squirrels" cards to successful tower climbers. Local Ranger Allen W. Stone of Park Rapids receives credit for creating the cards in 1927.

ONE WAY TO MOVE A CABIN: CUT IT IN HALF. The Aiton Heights Cabin was built by the CCC in 1941 to house fire spotters but was used infrequently. So in the winter of 1975, workers cut the cabin in half with a forestry chainsaw and removed it from its foundation. The foundation was so secure that it could not be broken up, just covered with a mound of dirt. The workers mounted the two halves on poplar skids, skidded them north to Lake Itasca, and reassembled the cabin at its present location by the boat landing. Jack Katzenmeyer, the truck driver who pulled the sections, recalled that the sections would start catching up to the truck on the steep hill down from Aiton Heights, and "Mary Hill was spooky." He would have to put extra power to the truck to straighten it out on those hills and on the curves on Main Park Drive to keep it from heading for the ditch. At one point, "it damn near ended up in Lake Itasca."

Aiton Heights Fire Tower

CLIMBING THE TOWER. Visitors climb the tower on a secure metal stairway surrounded by a cage. Interpretive signs point out the changes in flora and fauna as you ascend above the tree canopy, and the views from the top are spectacular. The Aiton Heights Trail itself runs east from the tower and parking area off Wilderness Drive, ending at Ozawindib Trail 0.3 mile south of Wilderness Drive.

TRAIL GUIDE

From Douglas Lodge, take Ozawindib Trail, which begins south of the main parking lot across the open lawn below the gravel parking area. Go across Wilderness Drive, where the trail leads down a long hill then up a longer series of hills to the start of Aiton Heights Trail.

0.5 At the Aiton Heights sign turn right, heading west. You will be walking through a mature maple-basswood forest, rich in wildflowers in spring and summer and the beauty of yellow, orange and red leaves in the fall.

0.9 Cross Deer Park Trail at the shelter and continue straight ahead. The trail drops down between Kasey and Allen Lakes, then climbs up a broad path, obviously once a road, to the tower. There is a picnic area and a rest spot at the base of the tower, elevation 1675', and interpretive signs. Return the way you came, or turn left at Deer Park Trail to return to the lodge, crossing Wilderness Drive and then turning right where Deer Park meets the Dr. Roberts Trail past the bottom of a steep hill.

Beaver Trail

Beaver Trail

Tucked into the forgotten northeast corner of Itasca State Park, the Beaver Trail makes a short loop through a dense spruce-and-fir forest east of LaSalle Creek. To get there, turn east on Clearwater County 4 (160th Street) from the Main Park Drive; go straight across MN-200, where the road becomes 400th St. Then, go east another 0.7 mile and turn right into the small parking area. Signage on this remote trail may vary and has been absent at times.

Distance/Time: 1.1-mile loop from parking area; 1 hour

Difficulty: Easy

Special Attractions: There are old beaver dams on LaSalle Creek, and the dense conifers attract woodpeckers

Hazards: Downed timber may obstruct the trail

Winter: 105th Ave. is a snowmobile trail. Beaver Trail would be a remote snowshoe trek

Facilities: None

Trailhead: Park in the wide spot on 105th Ave.

GPS at Trailhead: Parking area: N 47° 14.362' W 095° 09.174'; First (north) access point on 105th Ave.: N 47° 14.225' W 095° 09.188'; Second (south) access point on 105th Ave.: N 47° 14.100' W 095° 09.181'

TRAIL GUIDE

Beginning at the parking area, walk south on 105th Ave. 0.2 mile to the first access point or continue up the hill another 0.15 mile to the second, a wider open area to the right.

0.3 Beginning at the south or second (possibly unmarked) access point, turn right on a wide footpath into a mixed coniferous forest of mature jack pine, young white and red pines, spruce and balsam. As you approach LaSalle Creek, the trail bends north and drops down to a point where you can see the marshes and beaver dams in the wide creek bed. If you do pick your way out into the valley, watch for holes and washouts, as most of the dams are old and deteriorated, making for hazardous hiking. Enjoy the view over the quiet LaSalle valley. The creek meanders north through a chain of lakes, joining the Mississippi River just north of the new La Salle Lake State Recreation Area.

0.6 Continue north on the trail, which enters a dense stand of balsam fir, climbing a ridge overlooking the valley. The trail turns east, continuing back to 105th Ave.

0.9 Turn left (north) on 105th Ave. to return to the parking lot.

Big White Pine Trail and Big Red Pine/Bison Kill Site Trail

Big Red Pine Trail

As you travel around to the south side of Wilderness Drive, be sure to stop and enjoy these two spots. Each is a short and easy walk that highlights the natural and human history of Itasca, including the Bison Kill Site, which dates back to 8,000 years ago.

Distance/Time: White Pine: 250 feet one-way, Red Pine: 800 feet one-way; 15–30 minutes round-trip for each trail

Difficulty: Easy

Special Attractions: Examples of very old, large pines

Hazards: None

Winter: If you arrive here on skis or snowshoes, you could break trail to either site

Facilities: A small parking area on Wilderness Drive is available at both trails, with a vault toilet at the Big Red Pine trailhead

Trailheads: Big White Pine is 5.2 miles from the Mary Gibbs Headwaters Center; Big Red Pine is a mile farther

GPS at Big Red Pine Trailhead: N 47° 11.632' W 095° 13.901'; Big White Pine Trailhead: N 47° 11.809' W 095° 14.907'

TRAIL GUIDE

These two short trails on the southern stretch of Wilderness Drive lead to sites that are emblematic of the history of Itasca State Park. The white pine on the first trail, "Itasca's Largest White Pine Tree," represents one of the largest old-growth pines in the park; it likely took root over 300 years ago after a period of wildfires. Located on land that was purchased by the state early in the park's history, it was part of the 44 percent of the park area that escaped logging. Large groves of white pines were established after crown fires (fires that leap from treetop to treetop) had cleared the area, although individual trees are scattered through the forest, mixed in with stands of other species. White pine has gray, ridged bark, soft needles in clusters of five, and can live up to 450 years. Surrounded by a railing and viewing platform, the tree is a favorite photo opportunity as it towers over hardwoods and nearby pines.

Big White Pine Trail

MINNESOTA'S RECORD RED PINE AND AN ANCIENT BISON KILL SITE. Wilderness Drive winds around big red pines on its way to the next trail. Although the sign still proclaims it as "Minnesota's Record Red Pine," a storm in 2007 left the top of the tree bare and broken. It lives on, serving as a reminder that even the largest trees are vulnerable to the same forces of wind and fire that helped them take root. The red, or "Norway," pine has longer needles than the white pine, and its needles come in bundles of two. Norway pines can reach a height of 120'. The oldest in Minnesota is over 400 years old. The trail begins in a parking area near Nicollet Creek, the largest of the five streams that feed Lake Itasca. Proclaimed by Joseph Nicollet as the "Infant Mississippi" in 1836, the stream is fed by springs in the highlands along Nicollet Trail. It was here in 1937 that workers rebuilding this portion of Wilderness Drive found remnants of primitive bison, along with spear points and tools from the Archaic period, an archaeological designation dating back several thousand years. Detailed excavations in the 1960s showed that early hunters drove buffalo into the mire and then killed and processed the animals, which were much larger than today's plains bison.

BE ON THE LOOKOUT FOR INDIAN PIPE: A PLANT THAT LACKS CHLOROPHYLL. The trail to the big red pine is 800', a popular, easy hike by the wetlands of Nicollet Creek. Keep an eye out for wildflowers and other unusual plants. On the day I hiked here there was a small group of Indian pipe tucked next to a log. This white, waxy plant lives in partnership with a fungus and lacks chlorophyll, so it has no green color and feeds on decaying materials in the soil.

Blowdown Trail

Blowdown Trail

A severe wind-storm in 1995 ravaged 325,000 acres of forest in north-central Minnesota, knocking down mature pines and hardwoods in Itasca State Park and the sur-rounding area. Hills to the west of Wilderness Drive, exposed to the west wind sweeping across the valley below Lake Ozawindib, were particularly hard-hit. The Blowdown Trail traverses a stand made up primarily of mature aspen, which was leveled by the storm. These were saplings when the logged-over land was annexed to the park in 1919. After the blowdown, salvage logging removed the damaged and downed trees from one area, encouraging maximal aspen regeneration. Another portion was left alone to recover naturally, providing a contrast that illustrates the choices that are involved in managing a natural area. The debate whether to log dead and downed timber had once before come to a head in 1965, when the state legislature established the Wilderness Sanctuary directly across Wilderness Drive from here. This created an area where salvage logging would generally not occur, and damaged trees would be left to nature.

Distance/Time: 0.7-mile loop; 30 minutes

Difficulty: Easy

Special Attractions: Forest management demonstration with interpretive signs along the trail

Hazards: Fallen logs on trail

Winter: Generally not used in winter

Facilities: Parking; interpretive signs along trail

Trailhead: Landmark Trail parking lot and interpretive area on Wilderness Drive

GPS at Trailhead Parking Lot: N 47° 13.540' W 095° 15.319'

TRAIL GUIDE

0.0 The trail begins across the road from the Landmark Trail lot in a dense stand of young aspen and birch. This portion of the trail was logged to remove the dead and downed timber and shows how vigorously aspen regenerate when exposed to full sun. One quaking aspen tree can create suckers that sprout up to cover an acre or more. Bigtooth aspen and balsam poplar also reproduce primarily by suckers, which produce a clone of the parent. None of these trees typically reproduce via seedlings.

0.2 Where the trail forks, you may go either direction around the 0.3-mile loop that winds through logged and natural areas. Be prepared to step over a number of deteriorating logs in the areas that were left alone. Note the differences in the density, size and variety of the trees and vegetation in the two areas. Partway around the loop there is a pleasant view of wetlands south of Lake Ozawindib. The loop returns to the spur trail, which leads back to the parking lot.

Bohall Trail

Bohall Trail

Located on Wilderness Drive, Bohall Trail is midway down the western section of the park and enters the 2,000-acre Wilderness Sanctuary on its way to Bohall Lake. The magnificent stand of red (Norway) and white pine in this area is 100–300 years old, with some trees dating back to a fire in 1714. Other pine stands near Wilderness Drive were established after a series of fires in the early 1800s. Its scenic beauty rivals that of Preacher's Grove but occurs in a more remote and natural setting. Better yet, it is an easy trail to hike and sees only moderate use in the peak seasons.

A TRAIL WITH A LONG HISTORY. The lake was named for Henry Bohall, a rodman from Park Rapids on J. V. Brower's 1891 Itasca survey team. The trail, which reached east to Lake Itasca in the early years of the park, was originally used for fire patrols and to reach the West Station, a survey tower on high ground above the western shore of Lake Itasca.

Distance/Time: 0.5 mile, one-way; ½–1 hour round-trip

Difficulty: Easy

Special Attractions: Old-growth pines in the Wilderness Sanctuary, Bohall Lake views

Hazards: Blackberry branches in late summer, and a few exposed roots

Winter: Wilderness Drive groomed for skijoring, so Bohall Trail sees little use

Facilities: None

Trailhead: Parking area on Wilderness Drive, 3.8 miles from Headwaters area

GPS at Trailhead: N 47° 12.795' W 095° 15.314'

TRAIL GUIDE

The wide, mostly smooth footpath leads directly into a large stand of red and white pines. Lack of light and nutrients suppresses brush growth in a dense stand such as this, making it easier to see the majestic surroundings. Many years ago, there was a controlled burn here to clear underbrush and dead wood, which reduced the fuel available, helping prevent a more serious fire and also encouraging regrowth of pines. Note the black charred areas on the fire-resistant bark of the red pines. Older, hotter fires may have produced deeper scars that penetrated the bark.

0.2 A bench provides a quiet, cool place to rest by the marsh. There are also old hardwoods along this trail, and a fall hike will reveal flashes of red maples. May and June are good for orchids and other wildflowers.

0.5 The trail ends at another bench with a view of Bohall Lake and a broad marsh, as the shallow northern part of the lake has gradually been filling in with sedges and cattails. Beavers and muskrats have kept water trails open up to the old shoreline. As time goes on, this area will gradually become covered in grasses, and if undisturbed, eventually may transform into a forested swamp. Note the old white pines, which tower over other trees on the island near the eastern shore of Bohall Lake.

Brower Trail

Brower Trail

Named for Jacob V. Brower, the founder of Itasca State Park, Brower Trail is worthy of its name. Rich in wildflowers in spring and fall, it travels past Itasca's iconic sites: Schoolcraft's arrival point, Preacher's Grove and Peace Pipe Vista and ends at the Bear Paw Campground cabins. Begin the hike at the base of the Douglas Lodge stairway, wind along the East Arm of Lake Itasca, and climb to panoramic views well above the lake. The trail goes by some of the largest pines in the park, many over 250 years old. Bear Paw Campground is a good starting point for those camping there, and from there it's a beautiful evening walk to Peace Pipe Vista. For much of its length, the Brower Trail follows along a glacial esker, a winding ridge deposited by a stream beneath the glacier.

Distance/Time: 2.2 miles one-way, 1.1 miles to Peace Pipe Vista from either end; 1½–2 hours for the entire trail one-way, or a round-trip to Peace Pipe Vista from either end

Difficulty: Moderate

Special Attractions: Wildflowers, Lake Itasca views, Preacher's Grove, Peace Pipe Vista

Hazards: Rocky trail in spots; poison ivy from Douglas Lodge to Preacher's Grove

Winter: Hike or snowshoe, though Bear Paw Campground is closed in winter

Facilities: Restrooms, lodging, restaurant (seasonal) available in Douglas Lodge; fishing pier on Lake Itasca, small boat landing, Coborn's Cruises nearby

Trailhead: Begin just to the right of the base of the Douglas Lodge stairway

GPS at Trailhead: N 47° 11.545' W 095° 10.271'

TRAIL GUIDE

0.0 The trail leads to the right, just beyond the bottom of the CCC-era stairway leading down from Douglas Lodge. If you come in mid-June, a cluster of showy lady's slippers will welcome you. From there the boardwalk dives through brush and evergreens to a low, marshy area near the lake.

0.3 There are showy lady's slippers scattered along the marsh in spring, and closed gentians, intensely blue, bottle-like flowers, are found here in late August. You can walk down to the water near the big pines, but beyond this point there is no lake access. Above this area, on the cabin access road near Cabin 7, a plaque on a rock marks Schoolcraft's first view of Lake Itasca on July 13, 1832.

0.6 An uphill climb will bring you into the heart of Preacher's Grove, where you'll be surrounded by red (Norway) pines up to 300 years old, which sprouted after a fire in 1714. This natural cathedral, a frequent choice for weddings, is named for a preacher's convention that once camped here. The fire scars on the big pines date back to another fire 100 years ago, and show how fire-resistant the bark of these big trees can be. If pines survive a fire, they benefit, as the competing trees and brush are burned away, and the ground is left bare and pine seeds are more likely to successfully germinate. Enjoy a rest on one of the benches overlooking the lake or just stretch out on the grassy slope and take it all in.

1.1 Step onto the platform of Peace Pipe Vista and gaze out over the lake at a view that is part of nearly everyone's Itasca photo collection. Looking past the monarch of a white pine beyond the viewing platform, you can see all the way down the East Arm, past Yellow Head (Ozawindib) Point in the distance and to the western shore of Lake Itasca. At the top of the stairs there is a boulder with a plaque describing the geology of Minnesota. Parking is available here, making it a possible shuttle stop, and the bike trail is across the road and just up the hill. Large-flowered trilliums bloom around this area in early spring, and yellow lady's slippers abound in late May. Beyond Peace Pipe Vista the terrain continues to ascend and descend and the landscape ranges from moist ravines to drier high ground as you move into a younger forest. Bear Paw Campground is about a mile beyond this point, not 0.75 mile as the sign says.

2.2 The last part of the trail is a bit confusing, as there are several trail connections leading uphill to the cabins at Bear Paw, but stay along the widest portion of the trail along the lake and past the boat landing. The trail will eventually lead you uphill and to the right, meeting the campground road just past the first cabin.

GPS at this Trailhead: N 47° 13.015' W 095° 11.239'

CCC Forestry Demonstration Area

CCC Forestry Demonstration Trail

This short loop off Wilderness Drive highlights one forestry job tasked to the Civilian Conservation Corps in the 1930s: replanting pines in areas that had been logged in the early 1900s. The interpretive trail, developed in 1971, loops through 21,000 red pines and 5,500 white spruce planted from 1937 to 1940. This is a good place to get an idea of how a 75-year-old pine compares to the old-growth specimens on nearby trails. By the time the CCC completed its work in 1942, they had planted 124 million trees in Minnesota.

Take the interpretive loop to the left and read the signs as you go. Here you'll learn how the existing forest canopy, light, and soil types interact to determine which trees will thrive in a particular place. The trail begins in the pine plantation and moves through a mix of spruce and hardwoods.

Distance/Time: 0.4 mile loop; 15–30 minutes

Difficulty: Easy

Special Attractions: CCC plantation from the 1930s with interpretive signs

Hazards: None

Winter: None

Facilities: Parking area

Trailhead: Parking area on Wilderness Drive is a little over 4 miles from the Headwaters area

GPS at Trailhead: N 47° 12.520′ W 095° 15.406′

Deer Park Trail

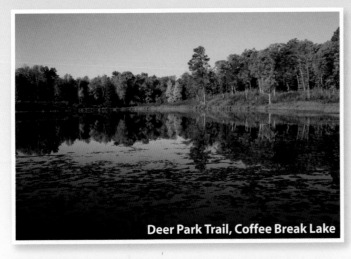

Deer Park Trail, Coffee Break Lake

From its start near Douglas Lodge, this wide trail leads south across Wilderness Drive, ending at Eagle Scout/ North Country Trail over 4 miles later. One of Itasca's earliest trails, its varied lakes and hills also make it one of the most scenic. The trail begins behind the Clubhouse, on the road to Cabin 11, sharing a track with the upland side of Dr. Roberts Trail for a short distance, before turning south (left) up the hill to Wilderness Drive. Deer Park has multiple connections to other trails, so the first 2 miles are often used as part of a loop.

Distance/Time: 4.3 miles one-way; up to 5 hours round-trip

Difficulty: Moderate to strenuous, depending on distance chosen

Special Attractions: Lake views, old-growth pines, one route to Aiton Heights Fire Tower, backcountry campsites (reservable, with a fee)

Hazards: The south connection with Eagle Scout/NCT is remote

Winter: The first 0.3 mile from Douglas Lodge to Wilderness Drive is snowshoeing only; the rest is groomed for classic skiing and is rated easy for the first 0.3 mile to Aiton Heights; after that it is more difficult to the DeSoto (McKay Lake) crossover, with the most difficult section spanning from the crossover junction to the Eagle Scout Trail/NCT

Facilities: Large all-season parking area and full facilities at Douglas Lodge in spring, summer and fall, with Forest Inn restrooms sometimes open during the winter; parking is also available near the Aiton Heights Fire Tower road off Wilderness Drive in summer

Trailhead: Start from the information kiosk near Douglas Lodge

GPS at Trailhead: N 47° 11.486' W 095° 10.378'

TRAIL GUIDE

From the information kiosk near Douglas Lodge, follow the sign to Deer Park Trail, which begins on a gravel road west of the lodge near the Clubhouse and Cabin 11. After a steep climb, the Dr. Roberts Trail continues straight ahead, so turn left (south) on Deer Park Trail. Climb another hill, and you will cross Wilderness Drive, entering the main part of the trail.

0.5 Deer Park Trail continues straight ahead, intersecting Aiton Heights Trail at the first shelter. You can turn right to make a side trip to the fire tower, 0.6 mile from here, or turn left to cross to Ozawindib Trail. The first part of the trail runs through a hardwood forest, with a few pines, which get bigger the farther south one travels.

1.0 Coffee Break Lake hosts the first campsite, a beautiful spot tucked into tall pines on the south shore of the lake. Surrounded by maples and pines, the tiny lake is especially scenic in the fall, the first in a chain of lakes to follow. Deer Park Lake is next.

1.4 Overlooking Deer Park Lake, turn east (left) here to reach Ozawindib Trail (the Hiking Club route) or for access to the three campsites on Myrtle Lake. The first campsite has some red pines; the other sites are more secluded and located on the point and are mostly surrounded by birches and brush. Deer Park Trail continues straight ahead, leading shortly to Deer Park Camp on your right.

2.3 After a long uphill climb to a ridge of maple and aspen and another short but steep hill, you reach the 0.4-mile crossover to DeSoto Trail heading right (east). As you continue south on Deer Park, the hills become steeper and the pines are older. There is a trail shelter with a fire ring across from McKay Lake, 0.2 mile south of the crossover on Deer Park Trail.

2.6 McKay Lake Camp is nestled in some gorgeous white pines. From here the trail follows a glacial ridge through huge sugar maples in this mixed old-growth forest, down a steep hill to a grove of white pines and on into a mix of old-growth red and white pines. Loons have nested on McKay Lake in the past.

3.3 to 3.5 A detour or side trail goes off to the right (west), but it's best to go straight ahead on the main trail. From this point on, a number of hills will make your legs burn whether you are hiking or skiing, and your neck could get sore from looking up at all of the big pines.

4.3 Here you'll meet the junction with Eagle Scout/NCT. If you head east, you are 2 miles from the Ozawindib/NCT Trail intersection, 5 miles from Douglas Lodge via Ozawindib or 3.3 miles from the South Entrance via the NCT. Westward it is 0.3 mile to the south end of DeSoto Trail, 0.8 mile to Nicollet Trail and a long way from Douglas Lodge via those routes, as you would have to walk (or drive the car that you left at a trailhead) back along Wilderness Drive from the trailhead of Nicollet or DeSoto.

Morrison Lake (pg. 108)

DeSoto Trail

DeSoto Trail, Picard Lakes

Beginning on Wilderness Drive 1 mile east of the Elk Lake boat landing, the DeSoto Trail leads to a trail shelter near Hernando DeSoto Lake and the Eagle Scout/North Country Trail. The 3-mile trail travels through a wide variety of forest types, mostly aspen and other hardwoods and some conifers less than 100 years old, and it makes a few forays into old-growth pine. It began as a forest fire management road to connect other trails, so it works well as a round-trip, if you return on Nicollet Trail or Deer Park Trail, a total of about 8 miles. You can hike a 4.3-mile loop by going down DeSoto, taking the Crossover Trail to Deer Park Trail and returning to Douglas Lodge via the Deer Park Trail. There are few lakes until you reach the south end of the trail, but sugar maple stands light up fall afternoons.

THE FIRST EUROPEAN TO SEE THE MISSISSIPPI. Hernando de Soto, the Spanish explorer and conquistador, is credited as the first European to discover the Mississippi River, crossing it near what is now Memphis, Tennessee, on May 8, 1541. (Alonso Álvarez de Pineda was assumed to have described the mouth of the Mississippi in 1519, but many historians now believe that his description is that of Mobile Bay and the Alabama River.)

Distance/Time: 3 miles one-way (3.5 miles to the Nicollet Trail intersection); 4 hours round-trip or more, depending on return route

Difficulty: Moderate

Special Attractions: Hernando DeSoto Lake at the end of the trail

Hazards: None

Winter: Groomed for skate and classic skiing, moderately difficult

Facilities: A shelter is available at the south end of the trail

Trailhead: Parking area on Wilderness Drive is 7.9 miles from Headwaters area

GPS at Trailhead: N 47° 11.391' W 095° 12.193'

TRAIL GUIDE

The trail is well groomed and maintained both summer and winter; about 10–12' wide throughout, it begins in a mixed hardwood forest of aspen, sugar maple, basswood and oak and follows along a ridge on the drainage separating Elk Lake to the west from the chain of lakes along Deer Park Trail to the east.

0.6 Old-growth pines line the trail until it reaches Clarke Lake. The lake, which may not be easy to see, is to the east.

1.6 A wide clearing at the bottom of the hill marks the intersection of Crossover Trail, which connects to Deer Park Trail, 0.4 mile to the east. To continue on the DeSoto Trail, go straight ahead. In the winter, Crossover and Deer Park are typically groomed for classic skiing only.

2.0 Marshes flank both sides of the trail, and there are some big white pines in this area. A beaver lodge is active in the wetland to the west, and you can see how the beavers have selectively cleared out aspen, their preferred food thanks to its soft wood and abundant succulent branches. The beavers leave the pine and birch to thrive.

2.8 The Picard Lakes are to the west; they are named after Antoine Auguelle Picard du Gay, who led Father Hennepin's exploration of the Mississippi River beyond St. Anthony Falls and present-day Minneapolis-St. Paul in 1680.

3.1 The trail shelter marks the intersection with the Eagle Scout/North Country Trail, which goes east from here, and connects with Deer Park in 0.3 mile and Ozawindib 2 miles beyond that. The trail to the west is still marked as DeSoto, though some maps show it just as the North Country Trail. In any case, it leads to the Nicollet Trail, and to the north there is also a shortcut to that trail that cuts off 0.4 mile around one of the Picard Lakes but misses Hernando DeSoto Lake and the ruins of DeSoto Cabin.

3.6 Nicollet Trail goes north at this intersection, and the North Country Trail continues west past the ruins of the DeSoto Cabin and two new backpack campsites on Hernando DeSoto Lake. DeSoto Cabin was a forestry cabin during the early days of Itasca State Park.

From this point, it is 4 miles to Wilderness Drive via the Nicollet Trail, 3.5 miles back along the DeSoto Trail, and 2.4 miles west along the North Country Trail to the parking lot north of MN-113 beyond Morrison Lake.

Dr. Roberts Trail

Dr. Roberts Trail, Showy Lady's Slippers

Showy lady's slippers, Minnesota's state flower, greet visitors to the Dr. Roberts Trail from mid-June to early July. A stunning display of these pink and white orchids flanks the trail at its beginning near the boat launch below Douglas Lodge. The trail, which officially begins at Mary Creek as it empties into Lake Itasca, winds its way through nearly every forest type found in this area. From the lakeshore you follow a boardwalk through a fragile bog area, then climb to higher ground near the Civilian Conservation Corps' Old Timer's Cabin, sheltered by white and red (Norway) pines. The cabin was built in 1934 of fallen pines so large that the walls are only four logs high. The trail, lined with ferns and horsetails in moist areas, goes up and down hills through a mixed forest and passes scenic Lyendecker Lake. From there it climbs to a higher and drier ridge, looping around through pines, dogwood and sugar maples to the beginning of the Deer Park Trail behind Douglas Lodge.

PLANT IDENTIFICATION MADE EASY. The trail is named in honor of Dr. Thomas S. Roberts (1858–1946), ornithologist and founder of the James Ford Bell Museum at the University of Minnesota. The late Ben Thoma, former park naturalist at Itasca, located and numbered 101 plants, trees and other sites along the trail and published a key with a paragraph describing each. His original booklet is still available for sale (the current price is only 75¢) or is available on loan to trail visitors. The booklet draws on Frances Densmore's work to describe American Indian uses of plants. Markers have recently been updated and relocated, and other resources are available to help identify the plants. The trail's yellow lady's slippers bloom in late May, before the showy lady's slippers take over in mid-June. These features help to make it one of Itasca's most popular hikes.

Distance/Time: 2-mile loop; 1–2 hours round-trip (first section to Old Timer's Cabin, 30 minutes, round-trip)

Difficulty: Easy and accessible boardwalk to Old Timer's Cabin, moderate with steeper hills beyond that

Special Attractions: Interpretive trail with numbered plants and booklet key, highly varied forest types and wildflowers, including lady's slippers, bog with boardwalks, Old Timer's Cabin.

Hazards: Boardwalks are very slippery when wet

Winter: This is a popular snowshoe trail

Facilities: Restrooms, lodging and a (seasonal) restaurant are available in Douglas Lodge; there is an outdoor toilet at the boat landing and a fishing pier on Lake Itasca

Trailhead: The trail begins near the Mary Creek inlet to Lake Itasca, by Coborn's Lake Itasca Cruise boat landing below Douglas Lodge; walk down the stairs to the lake from Douglas Lodge, or you can drive around and park near the landing, if space is available

GPS at Lakeshore Trailhead: N 47° 11.472' W 095° 10.703'

TRAIL GUIDE

0.0 Mary Creek and the lakeshore areas display lady's slippers in season, wild rice, cattails and other shoreline plants. The first section winds through a wetland, with distinctive trees, flowers and other plants characteristic of a northern peat bog. Please stay on the boardwalks that traverse these fragile areas.

0.3 The Old Timer's Cabin was built by the CCC in 1934 with huge logs harvested from Itasca's native white pines. Check for open hours and tours at the visitor center. Beyond the cabin the trail moves up ridges and back down through moist forest and wetland areas.

0.5 In July 2012 a storm blew down exposed stands of spruce and balsam fir on the hillside above Lake Itasca. The trail also traverses an area where a controlled burn was carried out several years ago to promote pine regeneration. The varied habitat in this section produces a wide range of wildflowers. As you leave the open areas you will begin to see maple, oak, paper birch and even yellow birch, which is more prevalent in eastern Minnesota.

0.9 A bench at Ray's Point provides an inviting overlook of the East Arm of Lake Itasca.

1.0 Lyendecker Lake is another beautiful spot to stop. You can either rest on the smooth rock or the bench that follows. The area is covered in red, white and jack pines and mixed hardwoods. On the south end of the lake, there is a beaver lodge. The lake was named after John Lyendecker, a surveyor and a frequent visitor to the Itasca area from 1888–1890.

1.2 The trail traverses a dry upland area marked by dogwood and blackberries in summer. Trail marker #75 leads in a few steps to an overlook that is hidden by foliage in midsummer. From the hillside above it, you can see a small glacial ice block lake, which has been gradually filling in with marshland. There has been beaver activity here also. A maple-basswood forest dominates this moderately hilly section of the trail, with large sugar and red maples providing beautiful fall color.

1.7 The Deer Park Trail joins the Dr. Roberts Trail here, with Deer Park leading to the right (south) up a steep hill to Wilderness Drive. To complete Dr. Roberts Trail, continue straight ahead.

1.8 The Dr. Roberts Trail ends on a gravel road. To continue, pick up the path heading to the right. It leads to the Douglas Lodge parking area, and if you continue to head to the right, it loops up and around the lodging facilities (0.2 mile). An alternate route leads across the high bridge behind the Clubhouse. To return to the boat landing area by Lake Itasca, take the short walk to the left that leads past Cabin 11 and down a stairway to the shoreline.

East Entrance CCC Section Corner Trail

CCC Section Corner

Distance/Time: 0.3 mile one-way, 30–45 minutes round-trip

Difficulty: Easy

Special Attractions: Unique CCC section corner

Hazards: Unmarked, unofficial trail

Winter: Snowmobile trail

Facilities: Near the Jacob V. Brower Visitor Center

Trailhead: Unmarked pullout on East Entrance (don't block the trail with your car), or walk east from Brower Visitor Center on the snowmobile trail, which can be confusing; it's best to have a GPS or online map if you go from there

GPS at East Entrance Pullout: N 47° 11.640' W 095° 09.300'; GPS at section corner: N 47° 11.762' W 095° 09.162'

An unmarked, gated trail located 0.4 mile east of Main Park Drive on East Entrance Road goes north, crossing the snowmobile trail to the Jacob V. Brower Visitor Center. Three concrete posts mark the entrance to the trail, which is likely a remnant of the Jefferson Highway era. Signs of the old roadway, its narrow ditches now filled with trees, are still present, but there are no signs of CCC Annex Camp #70, which was located not far from this site in 1933. Continue north 0.3 mile total and look to your right for the old split rock section corner, a few feet from the modern survey marker.

A MONUMENT TO THE CCC. Built by the Civilian Conservation Corps (CCC), the eight-foot-tall monument sits atop a concrete base, its faces pointing to the cardinal compass directions, with a small shelf indicating north. Despite weathering and deterioration, the stone rosettes and prominent arrowhead indicators on each face are still evident. Ben Thoma, a former park naturalist, noted that the CCC project to mark section corners in the park was begun in 1941, but the CCC program closed in 1942, so few were completed, this being the only known example in Itasca State Park. The trees here are a remarkable mix of young aspen and very old white and red pines, evidence that the CCC marker is located on what was the park boundary circa 1922.

The Headwaters Trail

Headwaters of the Mississippi

The Headwaters Area of the Mississippi River is the heart of Itasca State Park, the park's most popular attraction and the reason for its existence. Nearly every visitor to the park makes it here sooner or later. Here you can enjoy the river tumbling over the rocks at the outlet of Lake Itasca, hop across the rocks to the other side, walk over the log bridge, or even wade through the shallow water itself. But even this iconic treasure is a blend of human and natural forces.

THE HEADWATERS, TRANSFORMED. At the turn of the twentieth century, lumbermen straightened and flooded the original meandering, marshy outlet from Lake Itasca, damming the Mississippi River and raising the water level so they could float huge logs of virgin pine down the river. From 1933 to 1941 the Civilian Conservation Corps, beginning with Camp Itasca (SP–1), focused their efforts on restoring and improving the Headwaters. Using a 1901 map, they rerouted the first 2,000 feet of the Mississippi River to restore it to its original channel, covering swamps with 40,000 cubic yards of fill. Reshaping the landscape of 16 acres around the outlet, they planted a variety of trees to create a natural-looking setting. The rock dam is built on a foundation of concrete, with weathered rocks chosen and placed to look as natural as possible. After over 70 years of natural changes, growth and weathering, the spot has developed into the beloved place that it is today, enjoyed and remembered by generations of pilgrims to the Mississippi's source.

A SLIGHTLY LONGER MISSISSIPPI. The signpost announces that the Mississippi flows 2,552 miles to the Gulf of Mexico, which it once did. Due to Corps of Engineers channels and lower-Mississippi floods that have cut through oxbows, that number has gradually dropped over the years to its current 2,340 miles. It takes water over 90 days to make that journey.

Distance/Time: 800 feet one-way; ¼–1 hour or more, round-trip

Difficulty: Easy, accessible

Special Attractions: Mississippi Headwaters rocky crossing, interpretive signs, including the famous signpost

Hazards: None, unless you choose to be a rock hopper; be careful though, the rocks are slippery when wet!

Winter: Workers maintain the main trail from Mary Gibbs Mississippi Headwaters Center in the winter; you can also snowshoe or hike the short loop past Schoolcraft Trailhead, depending on the conditions; you can also ski here via the bike trail from Jacob V. Brower Visitor Center, which is groomed for classic skiing, and a snowmobile trail also reaches this point

Facilities: The Mary Gibbs Center has full facilities in summer. There are pit toilets near the Headwaters, just off the bike trail

Trailhead: Park at Mary Gibbs Center

GPS at Trailhead: N 47° 14.406' W 095° 12.637'

TRAIL GUIDE

From the Mary Gibbs Center, most people walk along the sidewalk to the left, where the main trail winds down to the Headwaters. The path is wide, smooth and easily accessible, leading across a new bridge and through conifers to the flat, sandy viewing area at the outlet. After enjoying the Headwaters, you can return the way you came or follow the path along the river that loops around over a different bridge, passing the beginning of Schoolcraft Trail on your way back to the Mary Gibbs Center.

To reach the Headwaters from the museum and picnic grounds, follow the trail leading north from the museum along Lake Itasca. Depending on where you begin, it will be a little over 0.25 mile.

The bike trail reaches the Headwaters along an old road, and there is a bike rack and a toilet a short distance away. You can snowmobile or ski right up to the Headwaters in winter, although the trails do not cross the river.

Landmark Interpretive Trail

Landmark Interpretive Trail

Itasca Wilderness Sanctuary Scientific and Natural Area begins just south of this short loop trail and covers the area bordered by Wilderness Drive and the west shoreline of Lake Itasca. First set aside as a natural area in 1939, this 1,600-acre area was formally designated a National Natural Landmark in 1965 and a State Scientific & Natural Area in 1982. Itasca State Park also manages another 400 acres as old-growth forest, so the Wilderness Sanctuary totals 2,000 acres in all. The trail celebrates its landmark heritage with a bronze plaque along a path that loops through a diverse forest just north of the SNA. This was one area of the park that mostly escaped logging during the park's early years, so the pines here range in age from 100–300 years old.

Distance/Time: 0.5-mile loop; 30 minutes

Difficulty: Easy

Special Attractions: Interpretive signs in parking area kiosk and along the trail

Hazards: None

Winter: A skijoring trail runs by on Wilderness Drive

Facilities: Parking

Trailhead: The parking area on Wilderness Drive shared with Blowdown Trail

GPS at Trailhead Parking Lot: N 47° 13.540' W 095° 15.319'

TRAIL GUIDE

This self-guided trail needs little introduction as it includes a dozen interpretive signs in addition to the kiosk in the parking lot. Note the information about controlled burns that have been conducted here to clear out underbrush and dead trees. This reduces the risk of future uncontrolled wildfires and encourages the natural process of pine stand regeneration. The windfalls here are evidence of storms from 1995 and 2012. The trail covers varied terrain despite its small size and traverses hills and several small wetlands. It runs through a variety of forest stands, from young aspen and birch copses, which sprouted in 1995, to ancient groves of red and white pines.

LaSalle Trail

LaSalle Trail, CCC Incinerator

This trail is in Itasca proper, and is not to be confused with the trails in La Salle Lake State Recreation Area to the north. The LaSalle Trail leads from the southeast corner of Pine Ridge campground and loops east through the forest, returning to the campground road 0.4 mile south of the camp. The maps of this trail can be confusing, showing remnants that are no longer maintained, although the signboards at the trailheads are accurate and the trail is clearly marked. It is a popular and convenient hike, especially for those staying in the campground. A trail also leads from the hostel to the campground and boat landing area.

A FAMOUS NAME. The trail is named for a seventeenth-century explorer of the Great Lakes and the lower Mississippi, René-Robert Cavelier, Sieur de La Salle. It shares the name of the nearby LaSalle lakes and river, and the new La Salle Lake State Recreation Area a few miles north of Itasca State Park (see page 52).

Distance/Time: 1.3 miles one-way (1.7-mile loop if you include the walk back to camp); 1 hour round-trip

Difficulty: Easy

Special Attractions: Spring wildflowers near Pine Ridge campground

Hazards: None

Winter: Snowshoeing

Facilities: Toilet, water and camping located at the trailhead

Trailhead: Park in the overflow area to the right as you enter the campground

GPS at Trailhead: N 47° 14.001' W 095° 11.368'

TRAIL GUIDE

The 10'-wide trail leads from the campground through a forest of mixed hard-woods scattered among old white and red pines, white spruce and balsam fir. The storm of July 2012 left a few fallen giant pines, oaks and aspen in its wake. Lady's slippers grace this part of the trail in spring and early summer. Remember that these wildflowers are protected and should not be picked or dug up.

0.5 The trail turns left here, and an unmaintained spur heads right, back to the campground road.

0.7 The main trail turns to the right through a mix of aspen, spruce and maple trees. A remnant of an old trail that is still shown on some maps travels straight, and it is mostly a deer trail, so it would be easy to get lost on this 0.3-mile dead end that finally leads to a nice grove of pines. The original LaSalle Trail once continued along this track all the way to MN-200.

1.0 The wetland to the south, a favorite of waterfowl, serves as a wastewater treatment pond.

1.3 The trail ends on Campground Road. Once you reach it, turn right and walk 0.4 mile back to Pine Ridge and the parking area. The gated, unmarked snowmobile trail partway back on your left connects to the Main Park Drive in 1.2 miles at the University of Minnesota Biological Station turnoff. It also leads to an old CCC incinerator in near-perfect condition, which is located 0.3 mile west of Campground Road, just beyond a power line. This trail is part of the original LaSalle Trail, that once went from the Biological Station all the way to MN-200.

Maadaadizi Trail

Maadaadizi Trail

"To begin a journey," the meaning for the Ojibwe name of this trail, expresses its purpose perfectly, as the walk behind the Jacob V. Brower Visitor Center is a great start for a first trip to Itasca. This accessible trail starts just behind the Brower Visitor Center and is a favorite of first-time visitors and photographers. Interpretive signs suggest other favorite trails within the park as well as explain some of the forces that have shaped the northern forest. Bird feeders on your way to the trail are busy, especially in the winter, so take some time to stand still a ways away and watch the chickadees and other forest birds enjoy a snack. Then, in a few steps, you will be walking in the shade of old red and white pines. Let your Itasca journey begin here.

Distance/Time: 0.5-mile loop; 30 minutes

Difficulty: Easy, accessible

Special Attractions: Quick access to big pines and some special woodland flowers, with interpretive signs along the trail

Hazards: None

Winter: Hike or snowshoe

Facilities: In the visitor center, there are restrooms, interpretive displays and a gift shop

HIKING GUIDE

Trailhead: Walk out of the Jacob V. Brower Visitor Center doors and follow the sidewalk to your right

TRAIL GUIDE

As you step into the forest, the dense grove of large red pines will likely catch your attention. Because the dense canopy keeps sunlight out, hardwoods like birch and aspen take advantage of any openings and fill in the gaps. Don't forget to look down, too, as spring flowers, like clintonia, a delicate greenish-yellow flower, are fairly common. Later in summer clintonia forms a bright blue berry (inedible), giving it the name Blue Bead Lily.

0.2 As you finish the first loop, cross the bike/ski trail to the next loop and enjoy some more old-growth pines. The trail loops back around in a figure eight to return to the visitor center. There are a number of dead trees near the end; these were left standing for the benefit of woodpeckers (including the Black-backed Woodpecker) and nuthatches, which feed on the bugs and worms that the deadwood harbors. Some trees are riddled with holes like Swiss cheese, and they provide valuable food and shelter to these birds.

Mary Lake Trail and Deer Exclosure

Mary Lake Trail

Beginning just a few steps from the Forest Inn, Mary Lake Trail disappears quickly into deep, old-growth forest. This footpath crosses Mary Creek and winds its way to the Mary Lake boat landing. The rest of the trail goes along the eastern shore of Mary Lake, providing panoramic views of the lake and the high hills to the west. With red and sugar maples lighting up the ridge in fall, this path is a real gem even though it runs near the South Entrance Road.

THE FIRST SETTLERS IN ITASCA. Mary Lake and Creek are named after Mary Turnbull, who was one of the first settlers in Itasca. She settled here in 1883 along with her husband, Peter. She also gave birth to the first white child in the Itasca area, Charles, in 1884.

THE DEER EXCLOSURE. The Deer Exclosure was a project of the Lovelis Lake Civilian Conservation Corps Camp in 1937. Due to overpopulation, the deer were starving in the winter, and they resorted to browsing from seedling trees so much so that pine regeneration was severely restricted. A fence was put up to exclude the deer from browsing in one area. The fence surrounded a 2.5-acre plot in a stand of mature red pines, which are now 270 years old. The deer population was reduced after hunting began in 1945, and the fence was eventually removed. The deer have continued to browse enough that it's easy to see where the boundary originally was. Inside, the forest recovered with a normal succession pattern of white pine, balsam fir, paper birch and red maple. Outside, the woods are still relatively open, with scattered young paper birch and red pine, lower on the deer's list of preferred foods, growing among the old red pines.

Distance/Time: 1.2 miles one-way; 2 hours round-trip, including the Deer Exclosure

Difficulty: Easy, except for the steep ascent to South Entrance Road

Special Attractions: Mary Lake views, spring wildflowers, Deer Exclosure

Hazards: None

Winter: This is a nice trail for snowshoeing, as it is convenient and lightly used; classic skiers can also return from Wilderness Drive to Forest Inn, but it is a chore for skate skiers, who will have an easier time on the groomed trail

Facilities: Forest Inn has ample parking, restrooms, and a gift shop, and Douglas Lodge is nearby with a restaurant and lodging (both facilities are seasonal); the trail can also be hiked from South Entrance Road at the Deer Exclosure or from the Mary Lake boat landing

Trailhead: Located just off the service road that runs around the south side of the Forest Inn; the large parking area is open year-round

GPS at Trailhead: N 47° 11.475' W 095° 10.126'

TRAIL GUIDE

Facing the Forest Inn entrance, the Mary Lake Trail begins on the service road to your right. Follow the footpath down through giant red pines in a quiet, moist forest and cross the bridge over tiny Mary Creek.

0.2 After a short walk, you will cross Wilderness Drive at the end of its one-way section and arrive at the Mary Lake boat ramp. The trail crosses a footbridge to the left, at the Mary Creek outlet, and runs along the east shore of Mary Lake.

0.4 Enjoy the view from the bench on the hillside. The trail continues meandering along the shoreline through beautiful red pines, until it climbs the steep bank to reach South Entrance Road, where there is a small parking spot. Continue across the road and take the few steps and the short hike up to the Deer Exclosure. It is a striking lesson in how natural processes interact in a forest.

Eagle Scout Trail/North Country Trail

Eagle Scout Trail, Gilfillan Lake

Eagle Scout Trail, which now incorporates a section of the North Country Trail, runs east-west, connecting the southern ends of DeSoto, Deer Park and Ozawindib Trails. The NCT continues east from the junction of Eagle Scout and Ozawindib Trails to the junction of the last bit of DeSoto/Eagle Scout and Nicollet Trails. Part of the historic Lind Saddle Trail, blazed in 1901, Eagle Scout Trail's name honors the Boy Scouts who once had a camp on Hernando DeSoto Lake. Eagle Scout Trail is quite hilly, but it's wide and well maintained, like the trails it connects to. Iron Corner Camp marks the junction of Hubbard, Becker and Clearwater Counties and was along the route of the first wagon road from Park Rapids to Itasca, which entered the south boundary of Itasca State Park near Frazier Lake.

Distance/Time: 2.4 miles one-way; 1½ hours, plus travel time on connections

Difficulty: Moderate, with steep hills in a few spots

Special Attractions: Beautiful views of Iron Corner, Gilfillan and Hernando DeSoto Lakes

Hazards: Remote trail

Winter: Usually groomed for skate and classic skiing, this difficult trail connects to the most difficult sections of Ozawindib and Deer Park Trails

Facilities: There is a backcountry campsite at Iron Corner Lake; for a small fee, it is reservable through the state park reservation office phone or on-line; there is a shelter at the NCT/Eagle Scout junction with DeSoto Trail

Trailhead: This trail connects with Ozawindib Trail on the east end and with DeSoto Trail on the west end

GPS at Trailhead: Ozawindib/North Country: N 47° 09.264' W 095° 10.242'; Eagle Scout/DeSoto: N 47° 09.101' W 095° 12.639'

TRAIL GUIDE Distances in miles, from east to west

0.0 This segment of the North Country Trail begins as the footpath from the South Entrance and meets the wide Ozawindib Trail. At the junction, there is a signboard and a map. Turn left to go south on Ozawindib and in 0.1 mile Eagle Scout Trail begins, and you will see Iron Corner Camp. Framed by a massive white pine on the north shore of Iron Corner Lake, it makes a beautiful picnic spot or a backcountry campsite.

0.6 A tipped-over cement monument from the old Lind Saddle Trail lies hidden in the weeds about 0.25 mile east of Gilfillan Lake. These concrete pyramidal structures once held wooden plaques marking mileage on the original horse trail that connected Mary Lake with Hernando DeSoto Lake. Governor John Lind paid $119.64 to construct the trail in 1899. This portion of the trail is hilly, and the ascent west of Gilfillan Lake makes for a nice rest stop.

1.1 The marshy north shore of Rat Lake is rich in wildflowers in summer. From here, Eagle Scout Trail enters majestic old white pines towering over spruce spires near Lashbrook Lake, then goes back into younger pine forest mixed with hardwoods.

2.1 Deer Park Trail angles north from here, traveling 4 miles to Douglas Lodge.

2.4 At its western terminus, Eagle Scout meets DeSoto Trail. There is a trail shelter here. Heading west, the DeSoto/North Country Trail intersects Nicollet Trail in 0.5 mile, with Hernando DeSoto Lake to the south.

Nicollet Trail

Nicollet Trail, Nicollet Cabin

Nicollet Trail travels 4 miles from Wilderness Drive to the intersection of DeSoto Trail, Eagle Scout Trail and the North Country Trail. The trails meet near Hernando DeSoto Lake and follow what was once the Lind Saddle Trail and a truck trail, traversing some of the most beautiful and historically interesting areas in the park. Most hikers just go to Nicollet Cabin or Whipple Lake before returning to the parking area. If you return the way you came, completing the trail results in a round-trip of 8 miles. If you combine it with a loop down DeSoto Trail (also an 8-mile round-trip), it is easiest to leave a vehicle at the Nicollet parking area, drive (or bike) to DeSoto, and hike from there, as Wilderness Drive is one-way from Nicollet to DeSoto trailheads. Or you can walk the 1.4 miles along the road in either direction. Biking is not permitted on hiking trails.

THE INFANT MISSISSIPPI. Joseph N. Nicollet (see page 207) explored and surveyed the creeks leading into Lake Itasca in 1836, four years after Schoolcraft's visit. He concluded, based on length of the stream and flow rate, that Nicollet Creek should be designated the "infant Mississippi."

Distance/Time: 3.8 miles one-way; 1½ hours (Nicollet Cabin and return) 5–6 hours (full round-trip)

Difficulty: Moderate, could be strenuous with long round-trip

Special Attractions: Nicollet Lake, the restored Nicollet Cabin, old-growth red and white pines, lake views

Hazards: The trail has a few rocks as you go south, and steep slopes and spruce thickets await those who choose to explore off the beaten path

Winter: Groomed for skate skiing, also used for classic skiing; moderately difficult

Facilities: There is a toilet just before the trail, at Big Red Pine trailhead, and 0.4 mile beyond, at Elk Lake landing; backpack camping is available at Whipple Lake (two sites), 2.0 miles south, and Hernando DeSoto Lake (two sites), 4.0 miles south; a reservation and a fee are required for camping

Trailhead: A parking area on Wilderness Drive, 6.5 miles from Headwaters area

GPS at Trailhead: N 47° 11.597' W 095° 13.743'

TRAIL GUIDE

The 12'-wide, well-groomed trail begins in a diverse forest of big pines, spruce, balsam fir, birch and aspen and follows Brower Ridge between Elk Lake to the east and the Nicollet Valley to the west. The first mile goes through old-growth forest, and you will walk through groves of huge red and white pines.

0.7 The trail follows high above Nicollet Lake (Nicollet's Middle Lake) with views of Nicollet Creek entering the lake through a tamarack swamp on the south end. A small spur leads to views at the edge of the steep, obstructed hill leading down to the lake. A beaver pond, part of Nicollet Springs, is just off the trail as you continue south of the lake.

1.2 Another grove of beautiful red pines surrounds the trail near Nicollet Cabin. First built as a forestry cabin in 1918, it was falling apart until its 1995 restoration by a dedicated group of volunteers. When we visited, a picnic table and two comfy outdoor chairs invited hikers to a welcome rest. A short path through spruce and balsam takes you down to the creek.

1.8 Floating Moss Lake connects to the boggy north end of Whipple Lake, named by Rev. Gilfillan for Bishop Henry Whipple, the first Episcopal bishop in

Minnesota. Whipple founded missions throughout the state, including the Breck School, originally in Wilder. His knowledge of Dakota and Ojibwe culture and advocacy on their behalf led to him serving as a mediator during and after the Dakota Conflict of 1862.

2.2 Whipple Lake Camp occupies a scenic spot on the shoreline, with two backpack sites, an "ax throwing tree" and a toilet. Some believe that these lakes represent Nicollet's Upper Lake; from here, the water flows underground to emerge in the springs that feed Nicollet Creek, but others think the upper lake is now a marsh.

3.1 Little Elk, McKenna and Picard Lakes provide a beautiful ending to your trek down Nicollet Trail.

3.6 A detour to DeSoto Trail heads east to the shelter at the intersection of the DeSoto and Eagle Scout/North Country Trail. This shortens the hike by 0.3 mile for those making this loop.

3.8 The DeSoto Cabin ruins lie just beyond the Nicollet/North Country Trail intersection. Hernando De Soto never made it this far north, of course, and the name commemorates his exploration of the lower Mississippi in 1541. It was built as a forestry cabin for fire control and forest management. There are two new backpack campsites just past the cabin on the north shore of Hernando DeSoto Lake, along with a toilet and stairs that lead to the lakeshore. This beautiful spot is directly across from Brower Island.

From the cabin ruins, the North Country Trail continues west and the DeSoto/ North Country Trail runs east to a shelter at the junction of Eagle Scout Trail. You can return back the way you came to the Nicollet Trail parking area or loop around to the east and then north about 3 miles on the DeSoto Trail, which ends on Wilderness Drive 1.4 miles beyond the Nicollet Trailhead.

Nicollet Cabin

North Country Trail—DeSoto Trail and Morrison Trail

NCT DeSoto to Morrison, Backcountry campsite

Until a few years ago, you could drive a 4x4 over the rough, rocky trail from MN-113 all the way to the south shore of Morrison Lake. A nearby resort would stash an old leaky rowboat back in the weeds for the use of their guests and other locals who knew about it. Today you would have to portage your own canoe over a mile to reach the lake, although it would be worth the effort to cruise along old-growth white pines that line the shores of Morrison, Bogus and Hernando DeSoto Lakes. The drive to the parking area goes north past the old Gartner farm, which is now an area of young red pines.

Morrison Lake is named for William Morrison, a trader who was most likely the first white man to visit Lake Itasca in 1804.

Distance/Time: 2.9 miles from the DeSoto/Eagle Scout Junction to 540th Ave. parking lot west of Morrison Lake; 2 hours one-way

Difficulty: Moderate (strenuous in winter)

Special Attractions: The old-growth timber and lakes are beautiful in all seasons, and there is lake access for paddlers who are willing to portage

Hazards: Remote area

Winter: Hiking and snowshoeing

Facilities: Parking lot; two backcountry campsites are located near the Nicollet/NCT junction; you can reserve them through Itasca State Park

Trailhead: The parking lot is located 5 miles west of US-71 on MN-113, then 0.5 mile north on 540th Ave., which is a bumpy sand road; in winter, the road is a snowmobile trail so you will have to walk from MN-113 to reach the trail

GPS: DeSoto/NCT/Eagle Scout, at trail shelter: N 47° 09.101′ W 095° 12.639′; Morrison Lake Trailhead, 540th Ave. parking lot off MN-113: N 47° 08.695′ W 095° 15.308′

TRAIL GUIDE

The trail guide continues to follow the North Country Trail from east to west, beginning this segment at the trail shelter on the DeSoto/Eagle Scout Junction, and continuing through the 540th Ave. parking lot beyond Morrison Lake. If you are hiking this trail from the 540th Ave. lot, from west to east, a short trail spur goes north, reaching the North Country Trail in 0.2 mile. Take the right fork to Morrison Lake and DeSoto Trail. The left fork goes straight and then bears west.

BEGINNING AT DESOTO/EAGLE SCOUT/NCT:

0.0 A trail shelter marks the junction of DeSoto and Eagle Scout Trails, with Eagle Scout ending here at a "T" junction with DeSoto Trail. (DeSoto Trail also goes north from here, returning to Wilderness Drive in 3.1 miles.) NCT hikers should continue west along the NCT/DeSoto Trail, staying on the main path between the Picard Lakes to the north, and a bay of Hernando DeSoto Lake to the south. (Don't take the detour to Nicollet Trail.)

0.5 DeSoto Cabin lies in ruins just beyond the Nicollet Trail junction. This old forestry cabin was used in the early days of the park but now is returning to the earth. From here the Nicollet Trail turns north, a 4-mile hike to Wilderness Drive; the NCT continues straight ahead to the west.

0.6 Two new backcountry campsites (#3 and #4) overlook Brower Island and beautiful Hernando DeSoto Lake. The campsites have fire rings, level tent sites, picnic tables and share a pit toilet. From here the trail crosses a short portage from McKenna Lake to the north and Hernando DeSoto Lake to the south, winding through majestic white and red pines.

1.1 Another set of short spur trails crosses between Hernando DeSoto Lake, now to the north of the trail, and Morrison Lake to the southwest. Shortly after

109

this trail you will climb a ridge and get your first view of the spindly pines and windswept sticks of Comber Island on Morrison Lake. The trail moves through a beautiful old-growth pine-and-hardwood forest on the ridge between the two lakes.

1.5 The trail drops down abruptly from the ridge, past piles of balsam and spruce windfalls, and crosses a marsh between Morrison and Horn Lakes.

1.7 The trail meets the old road to the marshy landing at Morrison Lake, a short distance to your right. If you do paddle around the many bays of Morrison Lake, you will find a small narrows on the west side of the lake that leads to Bogus Lake, which is ringed with mature white pines. The North Country Trail opens from a single footpath onto the wider old four-wheel-drive road, which is a bit rocky but still in old-growth red and white pines. Horn Lake is south of the trail, a tiny lake surrounded by large red pines. The otherwise open hillside suggests that beavers have cleaned out all the aspen. A short side trail on the northwest corner leads to a quiet overlook of this little gem, loaded with sunflowers in late summer.

2.7 To reach the 540th Ave. trailhead and the parking lot, turn left and go south down the straight path for 0.2 mile. Hikers who want to stay on the North Country Trail can turn right and continue to the north, toward Kirk Lake.

Two other short trails lead north from MN-113 on the south side of Itasca State Park. The trail just west of Frazier Lake is a trace of the old wagon road that led into the park in 1883 and was formerly known as the Little Mantrap Trail. Farther west, the DeSoto Lake Trail is a 0.5-mile trail to the southeast corner of Hernando DeSoto Lake.

North Country Trail—Hiking near Itasca State Park

Ozawindib Trail, original NCT route

On June 5, 1994, the first part of Itasca's NCT route was dedicated in a ceremony held at the Forest Inn. The segment ran from the East Entrance of Itasca State Park to Douglas Lodge, down Ozawindib Trail to Eagle Scout, and then to the western boundary of the park. At the time it was planned to go 3,200 miles, from Crown Point, NY, to Lake Sakakawea, ND, but since then the route has grown to 4,600 miles across seven states; the trail is being built and maintained by over 800 volunteers.

The Itasca Moraine Chapter of the North Country Trail Association maintains trails to the east of Itasca State Park, including scenic loops around Waboose Lake and other remote lakes in the Paul Bunyan State Forest. Similarly, the Laurentian Lakes Chapter has developed the trail west of the park, including a boardwalk through a wetland in Tamarac National Wildlife Refuge and several segments on the Laurentian Divide, such as the Tim-Don-Dell vista. For further information, see their *Guide to the North Country Trail in Minnesota* or visit their website at www.northcountrytrail.org.

HIKING GUIDE

North Country Trail—Morrison Trail to the Park's Western Boundary

NCT Morrison to West Boundary

As this segment of the North Country Trail winds its way west from the old Gartner Homestead, it follows the historic First Branch and Scenic Ridge Trails along a chain of lakes, all of them unnamed except for Kirk Lake. The trail begins in old-growth pine forest in this remote corner of Itasca State Park, then transitions to century-old hardwoods, as this entire western 2-mile strip of the park was logged prior to 1919. The western section of the trail has a beautiful stand of old-growth basswood. Built by a group from Bad Medicine Lake, it was one of the first NCT sections to be built near the park. Except for a few wet spots, the trails are level and smooth, a pleasure to walk on.

Distance/Time: 4.8 miles one-way; 3–4 hours one-way, 6 hours round-trip

Difficulty: Moderate (strenuous in winter)

Special Attractions: Remote area with solitude, multiple lakes, old-growth hardwood stand and fall colors

Hazards: A remote area, with windfalls and two confusing corners related to old roadbeds; follow the blue NCT markers! Ticks are abundant in the low, marshy crossings. Wear blaze orange during hunting season, especially on the westernmost mile of this segment, which is not in the park, and could be open to hunting earlier than the listed state park seasons

Winter: No access from Anchor Matson Road, except by snowmobile; the trail's remoteness and lack of foot traffic could make for a strenuous hike or snowshoeing trip

Facilities: Parking lot; the backcountry campsite near the west boundary of Itasca State Park is maintained by the Laurentian Lakes Chapter of the North Country Trail Association and is free and first-come, first-served; dispersed camping is not permitted within Itasca State Park

Trailhead: The Morrison Lake parking lot is located 5 miles west of US-71 on MN-113, then 0.5 mile north on a sand road, 540th Ave. For access to the west end of this segment in summer, use the North Country Trail parking lot on the west side of Anchor Matson Road, 2.8 miles north of MN-113; the trail begins just north of the parking area, ascending a bank above the road

GPS at Parking Lot on Anchor Matson Road: N 47° 10.357' W 095° 18.622'; GPS at Morrison Lake Trailhead: N 47° 08.695' W 095° 15.308'

TRAIL GUIDE

0.0 A short trail spur travels north from the parking lot, with its right fork leading to Morrison and Hernando DeSoto Lakes. Take the left fork, which runs straight ahead. The first trail segment begins on an old forest road, which is still shown on some maps and that used to go north all the way to the old Middlewest Cabin at the southwest corner of Wilderness Drive. It skirts the east side of Kirk Lake, which is named after T. H. Kirk, who wrote the *Illustrated History of Minnesota* in 1887. This segment is inside the original park boundary, so you will begin by walking through a grove of old red and white pines as you climb to a ridge with Kirk Lake to the south and a large wetland to the north. You may see signs of wolf activity in this area of the park.

1.0 You will reach a "T" with the old road that leads straight ahead. Take a left on the smaller trail, following the blue NCT blazes throughout. The trail drops down to a wetland and crosses over a boardwalk, the first of several in this stretch. Speckled alder, 10–15' high, is the most prominent tree around the marshes, and some are much bigger and older. In 0.5 mile you will walk through a wetland with ash, bur oak and quaking aspen.

1.8 As you cross the wetland, the peat bog to the south has leatherleaf and other acid-loving bog plants. The open-water marshland to the north consists predominantly of sedges, reeds and cattails. You will go by a number of unnamed lakes and marshes, and the trail may be wet in spots.

2.9 When you reach a trail junction, note that the road angling back to your left is gated, so stay straight ahead, angling right. You will reach the campsite in 0.25 mile via a short trail that goes down to the northwest corner of a beautiful little lake on your right, which has a white pine island amid scattered marshes. With a fire ring, a grill, log benches and a primitive toilet, the campsite sits on a flat area above the water. See if you can come up with some names for this unnamed little lake. Two trumpeter swans did a fly-by here on a recent spring hike, so you may see them in the future.

3.1 The wider road goes north to Ways Lake, but turn left (west) here, just beyond the campsite entry, on the narrower footpath of the newly constructed section of the North Country Trail. This can be easy to miss; the footpath is located at the following coordinates: N 47° 10.216' W 095° 17.094'. You will begin to see young basswood saplings, some stripped of their bark by porcupines, and you will soon enter a grove of old-growth basswood, sugar maple, red oak and large-toothed aspen. There are also some big white pines, and in spring the ground is covered with large-flowered bellwort, violets and hepatica.

4.1 Itasca State Park's western boundary is marked here, and you go from a narrow footpath to a century-old logging railroad grade that is marked by deep cuts and fills and gradual curves and elevation changes.

4.8 The trail presently hits Anchor Matson Road a short distance above the parking lot. Turn left and cross the road to the lot and North Country Trail kiosk, which has maps and other NCT information and alerts. Drive out of he parking lot, turning right (south) on Anchor Matson Road, 2.8 miles to MN-113, or you can turn left (north) and go about twice as far north to MN-200.

North Country Trail—
South Entrance Road to Ozawindib Trail

NCT South Entrance to Ozawindib Trail

Although the Itasca Moraine chapter of the North Country National Scenic Trail Association began building this trail in the early 2000s, it follows a historic route, as an Itasca State Park map from 1900 shows a trace of an old road here.

Distance/Time: 1.2 miles one-way; 2 hours round-trip

Difficulty: Moderate, hilly

Special Attractions: Sibilant and Iron Corner Lakes, access to Iron Corner Camp

Hazards: Some areas can get overgrown with blackberry bushes

Winter: Hiking and snowshoeing

Facilities: Parking and trail kiosk at South Entrance (State Park sticker required to park here)

Trailhead: South Entrance parking area; through-hikers on the North Country Trail will cross US-71 just south of here

GPS at Trailhead: South Entrance Road parking area: N 47° 09.253' W 095° 09.053'; Ozawindib junction: N 47° 09.264' W 095° 10.242

TRAIL GUIDE

The NCT crosses US-71 a few hundred feet south of the parking lot on South Entrance Road. A state park window sticker or a day pass is required to park in this lot. To access the trail from here, walk straight south from the kiosk, following the NCT signs across the parking lot, and take the footpath about 200 yards south to the NCT. Turn right (west) and continue across the snowmobile trail.

0.4 The blackberry bushes and stinging nettle that overgrow the trail from the swamp area to Sibilant Lake make for a prickly hike in late summer and fall, although the berries are delicious when they ripen in midsummer. Even though it has recently been developed, this is a historic trail, and it appears on some old state park maps.

0.7 Sibilant Lake is named for its shape, which resembles the letter "S." It is a beautiful sight to see in the fall when the white pines on the hills above it contrast with yellow maple and birch.

1.2 Continue left on Ozawindib to stay on NCT, and you will run into Eagle Scout Trail shortly and the Iron Corner backcountry campsite shortly thereafter. Note the signboard and map on Ozawindib Trail. If you turn right and head north on Ozawindib you are about 3 miles from Douglas Lodge or about 1 hilly mile from the Red Pine Trail, which leads back to the South Entrance Road.

Ozawindib Trail

Ozawindib Trail

From its beginnings on the broad grassy area just south of the Douglas Lodge parking lot, the Ozawindib Trail follows a historic route. Its hilly path along the west side of Mary Valley follows the first wagon road in the area, which was originally built in 1883 by Peter and Mary Turnbull and led from Park Rapids to Itasca. Mary Lake is named for her. This route led to the east side of Lake Itasca and had a major influence on the development of the park's buildings and intensive-use areas of the park, and it was used until the road along the east side of the valley was blazed a few years later. It was also part of the Lind Saddle Trail, and one of the saddle trail's original concrete markers still stands at the Myrtle Lake Crossover intersection. Because of its role in the early development of the park, it does not pass through solid areas of old pines, but its maples light up the trail in the fall, and there are scattered big pines, especially on the south end. It also connects with multiple trails and sees heavy use in all seasons of the year.

The trail is named for Ozawindib (Yellow Head), the Ojibwe who guided Schoolcraft to the headwaters of the Mississippi in 1832.

Distance/Time: 2.8 miles one-way; 4 hours round-trip

Difficulty: Moderate to strenuous

Special Attractions: Fall colors, Mary Lake views, winter skiing

Hazards: None; the trail is wide, mowed and groomed during all seasons

Winter: You will find some fun skiing on these hills, even the first part, which is labeled as easy; the trail is usually groomed for classic skiing as far as Red Pine Trail, then classic/skate skiing through Eagle Scout Trail; the south end of the trail is narrow for skate skiing, has challenging hills and is rated advanced

Facilities: Douglas Lodge and Forest Inn have restrooms, dining, shopping and lodging in the summer

Trailhead: Found in the vicinity of Douglas Lodge area, the trailhead is located across the open area south of the gravel parking lot and begins under some large white spruce trees

GPS at Trailhead: N 47° 11.429' W 095° 10.224'

TRAIL GUIDE

The trail begins just beyond the overflow lot south of Douglas Lodge, under some large spruce trees. The first short segment leads across Wilderness Drive, which is one of the primary routes that classic skiers use to access the winter trails south of Wilderness Drive. There was a major blowdown here in 1995, and the trees are still recovering, with new growth evident near the drive.

0.5 The old wagon road follows the western shore of Mary Lake, climbing through maples and mixed conifers to the Aiton Heights Trail. This trail leads to the tower, crossing Deer Park Trail along the way. The Ozawindib Trail continues south along the ridge above Mary Lake, becoming progressively hillier. Some big pines and aspen came down in this area in 1995, but the remaining hardwoods and spruce are spreading out and regenerating on the ridge to the west above the trail, so the damage is becoming less apparent over time.

1.4 The crossover to Deer Park Trail and its backcountry campsites via Myrtle Lake is well marked by a signboard. The Myrtle Lake Crossover also connects to the north end of Red Pine Trail in the summer. An old concrete pyramid remains from the Lind Saddle Trail, which was first planned from Mary Lake to Hernando DeSoto Lake in 1899. The monument originally had a wooden plaque on the side to mark the trail distance.

1.7 Okerson Heights Trail branches off to the right and is open in summer. Like other lakes in the Mary Valley chain, Deming, Arco and Josephine Lakes, all to the east, resulted from a series of washouts underneath the glacier that once covered this area. Over a period of time, water gouged out the steep-sided glacial valley between this ridge and the south entrance road.

2.0 A trail shelter marks the Red Pine Trail, which drops down into the valley between Arco and Josephine Lakes, then back up to the South Entrance Road. To the west, Red Pine Trail is open only in the summer, and it connects with the south end of Okerson Heights Trail a short distance from here. Continue south on Ozawindib, and you will find steeper hills and taller trees; the trail eventually encounters a nice grove of red and white pines.

3.0 The single track of the North Country Trail leads to the left, back toward US-71. To the right it merges with Eagle Scout Trail, which is wide and well-groomed like Ozawindib Trail and eventually connects next with Deer Park Trail, 2 miles west of here. Iron Corner Lake and its backcountry camp, just south of the trail junction, are named for an iron section corner that was once placed there in the early days of the Turnbull Wagon Road. The wagon road continued south to Park Rapids. The GPS location at NCT/Eagle Scout junction is N 47° 09.183' W 095° 10.204'.

Okerson Heights Trail

Okerson Heights Trail

A short trail between Red Pine and Ozawindib Trails, Okerson Heights is designated a "minimum maintenance" trail and is a narrow footpath that is only open in summer. Obstructed by

119

fallen trees at times, it is still well worth the effort, as it passes through a scenic area just below Okerson Heights, one of the highest points in the park.

Distance/Time: 0.5 mile one-way (or a loop of 1.6 miles via Red Pine and Ozawindib); 1-hour loop

Difficulty: Moderate

Special Attractions: Budd Lake view with its beautiful grove of white pines

Hazards: Blowdowns; infrequently maintained

Winter: Closed

Facilities: Trail shelter at the nearby Red Pine/Ozawindib intersection

Trailhead: Park at Red Pine Trail sign on South Entrance Road; trail shelter at Red Pine/Ozawindib intersection

GPS at Trailhead: Red Pine/Okerson intersection: N47° 09.862' W 095° 10.358'; Ozawindib/Okerson intersection: N 47° 10.166' W 095° 10.228'

TRAIL GUIDE

To reach Okerson Heights Trail take Red Pine Trail from its beginning on the South Entrance Road and cross Ozawindib Trail. Continue on Red Pine Trail up a long hill and you will see a sign for Okerson Heights Trail to the right, just over 0.3 mile from South Entrance Road. The trail traverses a beautiful stand of large white and red pines on a ridge above the east side of Budd Lake. From there it climbs a bit, then curves around the hillside of Okerson Heights to the west. After 0.5 mile, you will reach Ozawindib Trail. You can either return the way you came, or turn right (south) on Ozawindib, go 0.5 mile to the Red Pine Trail intersection, then left (east) to return to South Entrance Road.

Red Pine Trail

Red Pine Trail, Budd Lake

Red Pine Trail begins on the South Entrance Road and is not to be confused with Big Red Pine Trail on Wilderness Drive near the Nicollet Trail (see page 103). As its name suggests, it leads through stands of old-growth pine and connects to the Crossover Trail between Ozawindib and Deer Park Trails. The first short spur of Red Pine is open year-round, bringing skiers from South Entrance Road to Ozawindib in the winter, but most of Red Pine is a summer trail.

Several loops are possible from here:

- Red Pine Trail to the Crossover Trail, east to Ozawindib Trail and back south to Red Pine via Okerson Heights Trail (covers about 3 miles)

- A longer option would be Red Pine Trail to Crossover Trail, then west to Deer Park, north to Aiton Heights Trail, east to Ozawindib, then south back to Red Pine; this route covers about 5 miles

Distance/Time: 1.3 miles one-way; 2–4 hours, depending on loop chosen

Difficulty: Moderate

Special Attractions: Scenic view of Budd Lake, old-growth white and red pines in a park-like setting

Hazards: There is rocky footing in spots, and Red Pine Trail can be indistinct and hard to follow in the fall when all the leaves are down. A compass, GPS or smartphone would be useful; blowdowns may obstruct the trail at times

Winter: Closed, except for skate/classic skiing connection to Ozawindib, advanced

Facilities: Trail shelter at Ozawindib intersection

Trailhead: Park at Red Pine Trail sign on South Entrance Road; there is a trail shelter at Red Pine/Ozawindib intersection

GPS at Trailhead: N 47° 09.899' W 095° 09.996'

TRAIL GUIDE

Red Pine Trail begins as a wide trail that passes through big red pines between beautiful Arco and Josephine Lakes, two tiny lakes nestled in the deep valley south of Mary Lake. This wide part of the trail goes steeply downhill to a point between the lakes, each of which can be reached by short side trails, then climbs steeply back up to the shelter on Ozawindib Trail. Continue straight ahead on the footpath of Red Pine Trail.

0.3 Okerson Heights Trail goes to the north (right). Red Pine Trail continues straight ahead and winds around a few hills before it descends through a marsh to Budd Lake.

0.5 Budd Lake is surrounded by some nice white pines and can be accessed directly by a short trail through thick brush. The low spots on the trail may be overgrown by blackberries by late August. The trail goes up a rocky hillside as it leaves the lake.

0.7 As you enter a stand of maples and huge red and white pines, the forest opens up as the dense canopy above and the carpet of needles on the forest floor below have eliminated most brushy undergrowth. The track can be a little difficult to follow at times here, but it runs northwest at first and then generally northward up and down a series of ridges and ravines, until it climbs a hill and angles west toward Myrtle Lake.

1.1 From the overlook above Myrtle Lake, the trail descends to a wetland area and winds along the lake to the intersection of Crossover Trail at 1.3. From here turn left (northwest) to Deer Park Trail or right (east) to Ozawindib Trail.

Sawmill Trail

Sawmill Trail

A smooth, mowed grassy trail leads you to the historic Hemmerich Sawmill on the grounds of Lake Itasca Region Pioneer Farmers Village. Roy Hemmerich operated the mill on this site from 1952 to 1972, and it is now a major attraction when the grounds are open to the public on the third full weekend in August every year. Park naturalists lead tours to the sawmill and schedule demonstrations at other times, so check the program calendar for opportunities to see the sawmill in action.

Distance/Time: 0.6 mile one-way; 45 minutes to 1 hour, round-trip

Difficulty: Easy

Special Attractions: Pioneer Farmers Village

Hazards: None

Winter: Snowshoeing is an option, although part of this trail is used by snowmobiles

Facilities: Restrooms are available at the picnic grounds, near the parking area, and during events at the Pioneer Farmers Village

Trailhead: To reach the trailhead, go north on Main Park Drive past the picnic area and Wegmann Store, and then turn left (west) into the parking lot on Cemetery Cir., which is marked by the picnic area and the Indian Mounds sign; then, go around the outside of the lot to the left until you find the Sawmill Trail sign; the grassy field is sometimes used for archery demonstrations

GPS at Trailhead: N 47° 14.510' W 095° 12.139'

TRAIL GUIDE

Walk straight ahead on the wide trail, crossing Main Park Drive, and following the gated snowmobile trail to the power line at 0.4 mile. The snowmobile route turns left, but continue straight ahead through an open meadow surrounded by large white pines and bur oaks. Roy Hemmerich most recently occupied this old homestead, but the state removed the old buildings after purchasing the land many years ago. Bear left at a fork in the trail, and you will reach the sawmill at 0.6 mile and Katzenmeyer Avenue of Pioneer Village a short distance later.

Schoolcraft Trail

Schoolcraft Trail

Beginning at the Mary Gibbs Mississippi Headwaters Center, School-craft Trail is a pleasant, 2-mile round-trip along low hills and the old-growth forest of the northwest shore of Lake Itasca. The trail is great for avid birders, as it travels through varied terrain and forest cover along the lakeshore. On one morning trip in mid-September, our avian expert was able to identify 35 different species. These included the usual woodland residents, as well as several migratory warblers, gull species, and a belted kingfisher nesting in a sandbank. The trail ends with a view of Schoolcraft Island, where Henry Rowe Schoolcraft camped during his brief exploratory journey of 1832.

Distance/Time: 1.1 miles one-way; 1 hour round-trip

Difficulty: Easy

Special Attractions: Lake Itasca and Schoolcraft Island views, good bird watching

Hazards: None

Winter: Snowshoeing

Facilities: Mary Gibbs Center, open Memorial Day weekend through early October, has flush toilets, water, a gift shop and a cafeteria; it also has a large parking area and outdoor exhibits available year-round

Trailhead: From the parking area, turn right at Mary Gibbs Center; Schoolcraft Trail begins with a right turn before the Mississippi River bridge

GPS at Trailhead: N 47° 14.348' W 095° 12.593'

TRAIL GUIDE

The wide sand-and-gravel trail begins to the right of the bridge and is situated amid a moist forest of mature balsam fir and red pine. The trail was hit hard by the storm of July 3, 2012, which littered the forest floor with balsam fir and some pines in this area of the lake. Salvage logging has removed some of the fallen trees in order to reduce the risk of wildfire or pest infestations that can be spread by dead timber.

0.5 Enjoy the view of Lake Itasca from the bench here; the view looks across the north arm to the swimming beach. Wild rice beds stretch across the shallows of the lake, and gulls and waterfowl are commonly seen here. Wildflowers abound, especially in the fall, with asters and zigzag goldenrod blooming along the trail here and in the tamarack swamp just beyond.

0.7 After the first hill, you reach another area hit by the July 3 storm. While there is nothing pretty about the sight of a majestic white pine flattened by wind, the blowdown, which involved mostly smaller trees, created forest openings, which allow light to reach the forest floor and stimulate the growth of wildflowers, berries and young trees. As you continue on, another bench marks the point where the trail forms a loop around the last 0.25 mile. You may take the loop in either direction.

1.1 The trail ends on Hill Point overlooking Schoolcraft Island to the south. A fence encloses the mound of a small Indian cemetery on the point. The cool waters of French Creek enter the lake through the tamarack swamp to the west. The only Minnesota conifer that loses its needles in winter, tamaracks will begin turning gold in early October. Continue around the loop to return to the main trail. The inland segment of the loop goes close to a wetland area, where you can get a closer look at some tamaracks. They look like a spruce or fir but characteristically hold their soft needles in tufts of 15–35. They cannot live in the shade but thrive in nutrient-poor, acidic wetlands that are inhospitable for most other trees. Tamarack was the most abundant tree in Minnesota prior to settlement.

When you complete the loop, return on the main trail the same way you came. Turn left at the end of the trail to return to the Mary Gibbs Mississippi Headwaters Center, or turn right for an alternate trail along the Mississippi River to the Headwaters.

Two Spot Trail

Two Spot Trail

Named after the *Two Spot*—one of the Lima steam engines on the logging railroad that hauled logs from Lake Ozawindib to the now defunct town of Mallard to the northwest—the Two Spot Trail follows an old forestry road. The trail begins along the original western park boundary near the site of Middle West Cabin, an old forestry cabin that is now gone. It goes west through an area that was completely logged prior to 1919, when this section was added to the park. There are scattered old-growth white and red pines here, but most of the trail moves through aspen, birch, sugar maple and red maple, making it a great fall hike. Early spring and summer wildflowers are also an attraction.

Distance/Time: 2.2 miles one-way; 3 hours round-trip

Difficulty: Moderate to easy

Special Attractions: Historic logging road, spring wildflowers, fall color

Hazards: None

Winter: This is a skijoring and skate skiing trail, from the Wilderness Drive starting point about 2.6 miles north

Facilities: Parking for three or four cars is available at the trailhead, but avoid blocking the trail

Trailhead: Parking lot on Wilderness Drive, 5 miles from Headwaters area

GPS at Trailhead: N 47° 11.793' W 095° 15.293'

TRAIL GUIDE

The wide, well-groomed trail leads into a hardwood forest that is peppered with spruce and pines. Some of the pines have been growing since the end of the logging era and are over 100 years old, so even the younger trees look big now.

0.5 The trail goes up and down moderate hills as it passes by several shallow lakes and wetlands on both sides of the trail. Beavers have cleaned out most of the aspen around these lakes, leaving mostly birch and pine. The aspen can be seen towering over the lakes from the high ground above them, out of reach of the busy rodents. The trail is moist enough to hold wildflowers along the edges, and extensive large-flowered bellwort beds along the first mile provide a beautiful display in early spring. We also spotted a tiger salamander on one trip. The wetlands contrast with the higher and drier ground and have a completely different set of plants and flowers.

1.4 A wide marsh to the south of the trail leads to Dead Beaver Lake, surrounded by high hills. From here the path continues west through aspens and a few large pines, and its gentle curves and banks on the trail clearly identify it as an

127

old road in this section. Two Spot Trail ends at the western park boundary on Two Spot Lane forest road, which is a spur off the Anchor Matson Road about 0.5 mile farther west and part of the snowmobile trail network in the winter. There is an unmaintained trail that continues north and back east to South Twin Lake.

La Salle Lake SRA and SNA Hiking Trails

The hiking trails at LaSalle State Recreation Area (SRA) present a completely different look and tell different stories than those at Itasca State Park. The Challenge and River Overlook Trails are two-foot-wide paths, more primitive and uneven than the wide, mowed trails of Itasca. Hunter and Campground Trails, aligned on old roads, are 7' wide and relatively straight and easy to hike. The River Overlook Trail is the only trail that enters the Scientific and Natural Area (SNA), as it is managed for natural preservation and minimal human impact. La Salle Lake SRA is in its early stages of development, so there could be future changes—consult a current map when you visit. Except for the campground, the SRA and SNA are open to hunting and trapping, so wear blaze orange if you hike here during the fall hunting season.

Campground Trail

Campground Trail, Sugar Maples

This trail was adapted from an ATV trail that ran south from the parking lot along the eastern perimeter of the SRA and down through an eroded ravine to the lakeshore. The trail goes through a mixed hardwood forest, including red and sugar maples. Future campground expansion could change this trail a few years from now. The trail officially begins at the boat landing and runs along a path to the shower building in the campground, which is also a good starting point. It ends at its intersection with the Challenge Trail.

Distance/Time: 1.3 miles, boat landing to Challenge Trail intersection, or 1.75 miles to lakeshore via Spur Trail; 1½ to 3 hours round-trip.

Difficulty: Moderate

Special Attractions: Spring wildflowers, fall color, lake views

Hazards: Steep descent to the lakeshore if you take the Spur Trail

Winter: Snowshoeing

Facilities: Campground and picnic area with picnic shelter and restrooms

Trailhead: The Boat Landing has a small parking lot, or park in the Campground lot or Picnic Area (restrooms), which is a short walk over the bridge.

GPS at Trailhead: Boat Landing: N 47° 20.752' W 095° 9.834'; Campground (east parking lot): N 47° 20.625' W 095° 9.523'

TRAIL GUIDE

From the Boat Landing walk back up the entry road, turn right before you reach CR 9, and follow the crushed rock path that leads behind Black Bear and Lone Wolf cabins to the campground shower and laundry building, 0.3 miles. Then walk east to the campground entry road, turn right and cross the parking lot and open area.

0.5 You will follow the trail into a dense, windblown stand of young aspen, which have sprouted from the roots of existing trees after logging. Each group of aspen from a root system is a clone, with identical DNA, so there could be several clones in this patch of forest, or only one. Regenerating quickly after logging or wildfires, an aspen clone can live for thousands of years and spread over a large area. One clone in southern Utah, "Pando," is estimated to be 106 acres in size, contains 47,000 stems (mature aspen trees), and is tens of thousands of years old.

0.8 As you climb out of the aspen stand onto higher ground, turn right, and after a short distance the trail will turn left (south) again. There is a connector trail to Challenge Trail here. The trail now traverses a ridge high over LaSalle Lake, through a mature hardwood forest of maple, aspen and birch. Some were blown over by the storm in July 2012, which often happens to older aspen, as the trunk weakens about 20' up due to a fungal infection.

1.3 The trail ends where it meets the Challenge Trail. Turn left on the narrower Challenge Trail for 0.25 miles to reach the Spur Trail that goes straight ahead, descending a ravine bordered by red pine to the east. Eroded from prior ATV use, the drop down to the dry creek bed is steep at first but levels out with a gentle walk to the lakeshore, 1.75 miles from the boat landing trailhead, a pleasant spot to look for wildflowers in spring and early summer. The white kneeler found here appears to be a remnant of past weddings in this scenic meadow. You can return the way you came (3.5 miles round-trip), or use the return segment of the Challenge Trail to the campground and boat landing (3.8 miles round-trip). Or you may continue around the lake on the much longer Challenge Trail (6.8 miles round-trip).

Challenge Trail

Challenge Trail, glacial erratic boulder

Aptly named, this winding, hilly trail loops around LaSalle Lake, going up and down the steep ridge several times. Most of the trail is a 2'-wide footpath, narrower and rougher than the older trails. The trail goes through younger pines on the east side of the lake, then drops down through the LaSalle valley and back up, crossing the ridge on the west side before completing a loop around the entire lake. This guide begins at the Picnic Area on the west side of the lake. The trail may be hiked in either direction and can also serve to connect other trails as a shorter loop.

Distance/Time: 7.1-mile loop; 4–6 hours round-trip

Difficulty: Strenuous

Special Attractions: Lake views, wide variety of forest biomes

Hazards: The trail is new, with uneven footing, remote and narrow in spots; bring a walking stick

Winter: Backcountry snowshoeing

Facilities: Picnic area, restrooms, picnic shelter, large parking lot at the west entrance to the SRA

Trailhead: The trail begins in the Picnic Area at the west entrance to the SRA. The mileage guide begins at the kiosk here, although you can access this trail at several other points along the way.

GPS at Trailhead: N 47° 20.819' W 095° 10.073'

TRAIL GUIDE

Letters reflect current letter keys on the map of the SRA; bring an updated version, get one online, at the SRA, or at Itasca State Park.Beginning at the picnic area information kiosk, (D) walk past the picnic shelter and over the .LaSalle Creek bridge. Walk across the boat landing (E), past the steps leading to Black Bear Guest House, and through the first few spruce trees beyond. Here the trail climbs sharply uphill to your left, then turns right, where it runs through a blowdown area.

0.5 (F) A connector trail to the Campground turns left here. Follow the Challenge Trail straight ahead along the ridge above LaSalle Lake. The trail crosses ravines and winds around trees, taking a serpentine course through much of its length. It is a rougher, more challenging track, so the tread is uneven in spots and your toes will frequently bump on brush stubs and roots. The first mile presents vistas of LaSalle Lake through regenerating stands of white pine, a favorite target of deer in the winter.

0.9 Woodpeckers, which depend on standing dead trees for food and housing, have been busy in this dense grove of young white and red pine above the lake. A connector trail to Campground Trail (H) turns uphill here.

1.8 Campground Trail intersects and ends here (I). Challenge trail continues along the wide path to the right.

2.0 The wide spur to LaSalle Lake continues straight ahead, descending into the ravine. Challenge Trail turns left on a narrow footpath and winds through the pines above the ravine. As you go on, the trail enters thick "dog hair" aspen on county land that was logged a couple of decades ago.

2.4 An old ATV trail drops down the hill and intersects the hiking trail, but keep straight on the narrow path ahead as it continues generally south along the valley floor. The path winds around a ravine and several deadfalls, as it descends on a circuitous route to the creek bed.

2.9 You may find wet footing as you cross the sedge meadow of the creek bed. Both the wildflowers and stinging nettles are robust, so watch what you grab onto! The current crossing is a scramble across an old beaver dam and primitive log crossing to get over LaSalle Creek, but a bridge will someday span the area. After crossing LaSalle Creek, the trail climbs a ridge and turns north.

3.4 As you reenter the SRA along a sedge meadow you will walk among some mature aspen, whose rough, deeply grooved bark looks very different than that of younger aspen. The trail meanders in and out of county land, rejoining the SRA in a mature hardwood stand of maple, aspen and birch.

5.0 From a distant view high above LaSalle Lake, the trail drops down to a moist forest of spruce and balsam fir along the lakeshore. You can spot the black spruce by the dense clumps of branches that result because of the parasitic dwarf mistletoe that infests many of them, as well as a few balsam fir.

5.7 Here you will leave the narrow path for good, as you reach a wide trail on an old road. A faint trace of the old road continues straight ahead, but you will take the trail to the right after a short distance, at GPS point N 47° 19.975' W 095° 10.670'

6.0 The Challenge Trail officially ends here (L) as it intersects the Hunter Walking Trails. You will enter the southeast corner of the first of a series of open fields in the maze of Hunter Trails. Stay to the right and follow the wide trail exiting the northeast corner (M), where a Spur Trail (0.3 miles) leads down to LaSalle

Lake. A second prairie area (O) has a mix of grasses and scattered trees. Continue along the right side of the meadow until you reach a gravel road through the trees (P), the last segment of Challenge Trail to the picnic area.

7.1 You are back to your starting point at the picnic area information kiosk (D), which was once an old farmstead. A connection to the River Overlook Trail intersects near here, leading west.

Hunter Walking Trails

This 3-mile web of trails winds through two open fields high above LaSalle Lake and is more like what you might find in a wildlife management area. To reach the large north loop, follow the wide path to the Challenge Trail that leads up the hill and southwest from the picnic area (D) to the field (P). There are about 2 miles of trails here, including a connection to the River Overlook Trail. From the south end of the field (O) a 0.5-mile wooded trail leads to the southernmost 0.4-mile loop. This connects to the Challenge Trail (L) and 0.3-mile Spur Trail down to the west shore of LaSalle Lake (M). There is seasonal access with a small parking lot on Clearline Road (N).

River Overlook Trail

River Overlook Trail, Mississippi Valley Looking North

This trail through the La Salle Lake Scientific & Natural Area (SNA) north of Hubbard County 9 features a new path through the storm-battered jack pine forest, so you can follow its recovery from the July 2012 windstorm. The sudden exposure to light has sparked an explosion of wild-flowers, which are especially beautiful in early fall.

Distance/Time: 1.1 miles from SRA day-use area or 0.7 mile from SNA lot; 1 hour round-trip

Difficulty: Easy

Special Attractions: Scenic view of the LaSalle Creek confluence with the Mississippi River

Hazards: Uneven footing in places

Winter: Snowshoeing

Facilities: La Salle Lake SRA day-use area, picnic shelter and restrooms

Trailhead: The trail leaves from the northwest corner of the day-use area parking lot. You can also park in the SNA parking lot on the north side of Hubbard County 9

GPS at Trailhead: Day-use area kiosk: N 47° 20.819' W 095° 10.073'; SNA parking lot on Hubbard County: 9 N 47° 20.984' W 095° 10.380'

TRAIL GUIDE

The trail guide begins near the northwest corner of the day-use picnic area in the west entrance to the SRA. Heading west, the trail enters the woods and then emerges into an open area of regenerating forest.

0.3 The wider Hunter Trail branches off to the left and curves up a slope; continue straight ahead on the River Overlook Trail, which turns north and crosses the county road.

0.4 From the small parking lot at the SNA boundary, the path goes along the right side of the old field, then turns right in less than 0.1 mile. As you enter the blowdown, you can see the few spindly jack pines that survived the storm, remnants of the solid stand that had covered the entire area. The damaged trees were cleared to remove the potential reservoir of jack pine budworm, reduce fire danger and hasten regeneration. On the fall day that I walked through here, the reddish browns of brush and ferns and the explosion of asters, goldenrod and pearly everlasting made the hike surprisingly beautiful.

0.8 A grove of red pine frames your view of LaSalle Creek, which winds through a broad marsh on its way to the Mississippi River. Head back inland, and you will be surrounded by a stand of balsam poplar saplings that shot up over six feet in their first year. The abundant chlorophyll in their huge leaves and even their bark helps them outcompete everything else around.

1.1 As you approach the point above the confluence, you will at last see a few jack pine survivors. Enjoy the view up and down the young Mississippi Valley and its confluence with LaSalle Creek, which enters to your right.

North Country Trail, West of Morrison Lake

Waboose Lake, North Country Trail

Deer Park Trail

Cross-country Skiing in Itasca

Here is a sampler of the nearly 31 miles of groomed trails that Itasca State Park boasts.

A cross-country skiing destination, Itasca State Park grooms trails for classic skiing, skate skiing, or both. With the addition of the beginner-friendly South Entrance Road and a skijoring trail on the west side of Wilderness Drive, the park maintains options for every level of skiing expertise and interest. Grooming trails can be difficult for park personnel due to the remoteness and steepness of some of the trails, especially in adverse weather, and you may sometimes need to break trail or adapt to changing snow conditions. The Jacob V. Brower Visitor Center keeps an updated log of trail grooming activity and conditions, which is also posted regularly on Itasca's DNR website.

Eagle Scout Trail

South Entrance Road Ski Trail

South Entrance Road: Groomed for skate and classic skiing, the gentle hills and curves make this the perfect trail to learn new techniques or get in a relaxed rhythm. The entire road, from the East Entrance station to the South Entrance of the park, is blocked off. It is groomed at least to Red Pine Trail, which connects to Ozawindib Trail.

Bike Trail to Headwaters: Leaving from Douglas Lodge with two classic tracks, the 6-mile trail (each way) goes near Preacher's Grove, Peace Pipe Vista and other sites along the way. Groomed over asphalt like the South Entrance Road, but narrower, it is a smooth, moderately hilly cruise ending at the Mary Gibbs Mississippi Headwaters Center and the Headwaters. That center is closed in winter, but the parking lot and trail to the Headwaters are plowed.

Wilderness Drive, Mary Lake

Wilderness Drive: The Wilderness Drive loop from the Mary Lake area through Nicollet Trail is groomed for skate/classic skiing. Access is via the South Entrance Road or the first section of Ozawindib Trail. South of the Lake Ozawindib access road, Wilderness Drive is groomed for skijoring and skate skiing (and this includes Two Spot Trail).

Ozawindib Trail: The northern half to Red Pine Trail is groomed for classic skiing; a skate lane is added south of that. That part is a bit narrower than the other skate trails and can be a handful in fast or icy conditions.

SKIING GUIDE

140

Deer Park Trail

Deer Park/Aiton Heights Trails:
The north ends of these classic
trails are relatively close to the
lodge, easy and well traveled.
Aiton Heights Trail cuts across
Deer Park to Ozawindib Trail,
providing options for a short
loop. South of that, Deer Park has
intermediate hills, with a cross-
over to Ozawindib east at Myrtle Lake and, beyond that, a crossover
west to DeSoto Trail. Deer Park continues south to Eagle Scout and gets
steeper as it progresses, with the last 1.8 miles rated advanced.

DeSoto Trail: This classic/skating intermediate trail goes through hardwoods initially but leads into old-growth pines as it nears Eagle Scout
Trail. The classic crossover to Deer Park, noted above, provides a loop
of about 6 miles; if you take the entire Wilderness-DeSoto-Eagle
Scout-Deer Park loop, it is 9 miles.

Nicollet Trail: Packed for intermediate level skating, but used by classic
skiers as well, the Nicollet Trail begins in the pines along Brower Ridge
and passes near several lakes, ending at Hernando DeSoto Lake near
DeSoto Trail. A complete loop of Wilderness Drive-Nicollet-Eagle
Scout-Ozawindib-Red Pine-South Entrance Road is about 13 miles.

Eagle Scout: Tracked for skating/classic, this route connects the southern
end of the trails coming off Wilderness Drive. The 1.9 miles from Deer
Park Trail to Ozawindib Trail are rated advanced and take a little longer
than you might expect.

SKIING GUIDE

Wilderness Drive

A Guided Driving Tour of Itasca

This is your guided tour to driving through Itasca State Park.

Ever since its years as a prized stop along the Jefferson Highway, Itasca has been known for its scenic drives. Now a part of the Lake Country Scenic Byway, which stretches from Detroit Lakes to Walker along MN-34 and from Park Rapids to Itasca along US-71, the roads around Itasca are noted for their beauty during all seasons of the year.

Wilderness Drive

Peace Pipe Vista

Scenic Drives, Sights to See and Superb Structures

DRIVING TOUR

East Entrance

EAST ENTRANCE

The classic Civilian Conservation Corps era sign welcomes you to a park that has been impacted by human habitation since its beginnings. Even amid the old-growth red and white pines of the East Entrance, it's not hard to see effects of a controlled burn. This was done several years ago to clear out brush to encourage pine regeneration and also to reduce the fuel load from dead trees and branches that could trigger a more severe fire

144

in dry conditions. At 0.6 mile from MN-200, you cross a glacial esker, a winding ridge that angles across the road through the woods. When you reach the South Entrance Road intersection, turn right for the entry station.

Josephine Lake

SOUTH ENTRANCE

A popular entry point for those coming from the south, this beautiful drive leads you through a series of deep lakes in Mary Valley, which is a glacial tunnel valley that extends from the southeast corner of the park up through Lake Itasca's East Arm. After a series of wetlands, you will see Josephine Lake, named after Josephine Brower, and Arco Lake, after Michel Accault, who led Father Hennepin's trip to St. Anthony Falls and beyond in 1680. Red Pine Trail begins here, dropping down between the two lakes into the steep valley. Next comes Deming Lake, named after Portius C. Deming, an early park advocate.

Mary Lake is known for beautiful views, especially in fall, as maples light up the hills. Hike up to the Deer Exclosure near the end of Mary Lake Trail midway along the lake. A wide area of ancient forest runs from Deming Lake through East Entrance Road. If the entry station for permits and information just beyond that is closed, proceed to the Jacob V. Brower Visitor Center.

South Entrance Road is closed in winter, when it is transformed into a beautifully groomed ski trail. Your navigation device may not be aware that the road is impassable, so if you see snowdrifts, use the East Entrance!

DRIVING TOUR

145

Jacob V. Brower Visitor Center

JACOB V. BROWER VISITOR CENTER

The most intensively visited area of the park is just past the entry station. The Jacob V. Brower Visitor Center on your right has two parking lots and a large vehicle/overflow lot. Bicyclists should park and unload bikes in the lot just beyond the Visitor Center. The vaulted beamed ceiling covers a lobby area, a gift shop, restrooms and an information station with maps and brochures of park and nearby attractions. A huge trumpeter swan welcomes you to the extensive displays, which cover everything you will want to know about the history, layout and natural wonders of the Itasca area. Beyond the 3-D map of Itasca, you can take a video tour of the park, and kids and adults will enjoy the stuffed birds, the Indian wigwam and other hands-on and interactive stations. Wi-Fi is available here and at Douglas Lodge. The center is open year-round.

DRIVING TOUR

Douglas Lodge

DOUGLAS LODGE AND FOREST INN

Douglas Lodge and Forest Inn are a short drive away, or can be reached via the bike trail. Douglas Lodge, dedicated in 1905, is the oldest building still standing in Itasca. It was constructed by T. C. and Samuel Myers of Park Rapids and built in the Rustic Style popular with national parks of its era. The restaurant is open late May through early October, serving breakfast, lunch and dinner, and it features dishes with a Minnesota theme. Their wild rice soup, salads, casseroles, blueberry malts and bison burgers all use local foods, and even their wine and beer list is exclusively Minnesotan. The lobby has changed little since 1905 and remains a cozy spot to read or relax. Forest Inn, the gem completed by the Veteran's Conservation Corps in 1941 (see Itasca History) is a log and stone structure that houses a modern gift shop and bookstore that sells clothing, vintage reproductions of early Minnesota china and other wares. The warm entry, with its expertly made masonry and woodwork, is carefully preserved and close to its original condition. The room to your right has a grand fireplace and tables for informal indoor picnics. It can be reserved for weddings, receptions and private gatherings.

DRIVING TOUR

147

Coborn's Lake Itasca Tours

COBORN'S LAKE ITASCA TOURS

The Coborn family has been leading boat tours on Lake Itasca since 1985. Their current vessel, the *Chester Charles II,* takes you on a 10-mile, 2-hour tour of the lake. Tours are available from Memorial Day through early October. Featuring loons, frequent sightings of bald eagles and other wildlife, the naturalist-narrated tours leave from the dock below Douglas Lodge. Lakeside parking is available. Special Buffet Dinner evenings are featured in midsummer and are catered by Douglas Lodge; and you can charter the boat for private events and even weddings. For more information, visit: http://www.lakeitascatours.com/index.html

You can walk down the Douglas Lodge stairs to reach Coborn's dock, or you can drive there. To drive, head straight through the parking lot, turn right on the road that curves around past the overflow lot, then turn left behind Douglas Lodge, and follow the signs down to the boat landing parking area.

MAIN PARK DRIVE

Main Park Drive connects the most popular sites and facilities in the park and leads to the Headwaters in less than 5 miles. The road is smooth but narrow and winding, with a 30 mph speed limit that is well above the pace of traffic you might find on a busy summer afternoon. Watch for pedestrians, bikers, wide RVs and campers and slow traffic along the entire route, which is peppered with yellow lady's slippers and other wildflowers in season. From a high bank over Lake Itasca's East Arm, you will enjoy views of the lake through large white and red pines, many of which are over 300 years old.

DRIVING TOUR

Preacher's Grove, named for its cathedral-like setting and for a preachers' convention once held here, is still the site of preaching during summer weddings. Its majestic grove of red pines grew up here after major fires in the early 1700s, and scars on their fire-resistant bark date to more recent blazes, the latest being over 100 years ago. Farther on you will drive through some areas that were clear-cut in the early 1900s and have now grown back into a mixed forest of mature aspen, maple and younger red and white pines. (If you want to stop here, there is a parking lot on the east side of the road.)

Peace Pipe Vista looks across the East Arm of Lake Itasca. The steep stairway crosses Brower Trail and leads to a deck with an iconic view of the lake. Peace Pipe Springs, named for the "piece of pipe" that stuck out of the bank to facilitate water collection, trickles into the lake from the steep bank below. After Peace Pipe, the road runs through an open stand of red pine, then moves into a younger forest of pine mixed with aspen and other hardwoods. A storm on July 2, 2012, blew down a number of trees, including some old pines, in an area from here up to the Headwaters. (There is a well-marked parking area on the west side of Main Park Drive, and it leads to the overlook.)

Campground Road is next, with Bear Paw to the left and Pine Ridge and Campground Office to your right, open May through October. Campers heading for either site should register at the Campground Office. (Winter campers at Pine Ridge should continue on and take a right turn near the boat landing and register at the Jacob V. Brower Visitor Center.)

The next left leads to the University of Minnesota Itasca Biological Station and Laboratories. Educating its first forestry students in 1909, the station welcomes field biology students, researchers and educational groups during the summer months. A separate entity from Itasca State Park, it has inspired generations of young scientists, and its research has proven valuable in guiding park management decisions. Construction of a new campus center began in April 2013.

Pioneer Cemetery, protected by a simple rail fence, was established on land donated by William McMullen. It holds his remains and those of thirteen other

149

early settlers to the Itasca area, including Theodore and Johanna Wegmann. There are seven people interred here under the age of ten, the first being nine-year-old Luise Rorich, daughter of a homesteader. It can be reached by a short bike ride or a walk south from the boat landing.

Lake Itasca Boat Landing

THE BOAT LANDING AND THE BEACH

The boat landing on Lake Itasca has a double boat ramp, a fish cleaning house and a spacious parking lot that can be nearly filled during fishing opener and other peak fishing and boating times. Itasca Sports rents bikes, boats, canoes, kayaks, pontoons, fishing equipment and related gear (see page 42). Headwaters Hostel is across Main Park Drive and a short drive up Forest Lane (see page 28).

The picnic grounds, swimming beach and museum cover a wide area along the northeast shore of Lake Itasca. There are several parking lots that stretch from the swimming beach and through the picnic grounds to the museum and amphitheater area and the Wegmann Store. You can drive all the way through these lots and enter from either the north or south end of the area.

The beautiful sand beach, still a hotspot on hot summer days, has a 1940s log changing house, a volleyball net and picnic tables. The nearby grounds have been the site of family picnics and group gatherings for decades. A large picnic shelter sits above the lake, with tables and fire pit grills throughout the area. The museum holds interpretive displays featuring local and Indian tribal history, and a small amphitheater nearby may ring with folk music on summer evenings, a band concert in early June, or an informal church service on Sunday mornings. As you walk around the grounds toward the Headwaters, interpretive signs tell stories of Itasca's early settlers.

As you continue toward the Headwaters, you'll encounter the Wegmann Store ruins. Theodore and Johanna Wegmann homesteaded on their Lake Itasca property in 1893 and later built a store, serving tourists and local customers with lodging and groceries into the 1930s. A replica of the Wegmann Store has been built near the crumbling ruins of the original store. Dorothy Welle, who lived in Arago (near the present-day town of Two Inlets), recalls the days when they would bring ice cream from Park Rapids, frozen in dry ice. "They had ice cream and tables and chairs, just like a soda fountain. We were poor, and every Christmas we would get a bag of every kind of nut they had in the store and half a bag of candy. It was a beautiful place, and they were wonderful people." The pond nearby is popular with ducks, frogs and turtles, and the woods shelter spring wildflowers. Continue walking toward the Headwaters for a trip to the log-and-stone CCC-era latrine.

Turn west on Cemetery Lane to reach the parking area for the Indian Cemetery, which is located on the other side of the wetland from the Wegmann Store. The Indian Cemetery burial mounds are a short walk from here. Jacob Brower found his first hint of prehistoric occupation here while he camped on today's picnic grounds in 1894. He awoke one morning to find a pottery sherd that had been tossed up by a pocket gopher. Brower was familiar with the pattern, and the discovery led to his further excavations of the old Indian villages along the shore and his excavation and reconstruction of nine of the ten burial mounds in 1895. Brower wrote, "thus the little mound-builder . . . unconsciously brought to light the existence of the ancient mound-builder . . . who preceded this particular one by many centuries at the source of the Mississippi." The burial mounds, which date back to Late Woodland Indians, about 500–900 years ago, lie behind a rail fence a short distance from the parking lot.

At the intersection of Clearwater County 117 (Wilderness Drive) and Clearwater County 122 (North Entrance Drive), follow Clearwater County 117 straight ahead across the new bridge over the Mississippi River to the Mary Gibbs Mississippi Headwaters Center and Wilderness Drive, which begins there. To exit the park via the North Entrance, turn right on 122 and go 0.5 mile to MN-200.

Lake Itasca Region Pioneer Farmers

NORTH ENTRANCE

For park entry from the north, via MN-200, turn south on Clearwater County 122 and drive past Rock Creek General Store. St. Catherine's Catholic Church, now a closed parish, still provides a Sunday 9 a.m. mass during the summer months, with visiting priests from all over the country, and it has held a special hunters' mass at 5:30 a.m. on opening day of deer hunting season. Anita Willet, who was married to Jerry there 62 years ago, remembers watching Father Fraling high up on scaffolding, stenciling the intricate designs you can still see today. The old Lake Itasca Post Office and store have long since closed. The Lake Itasca Region Pioneer Farmers, located just south of the entrance on MN-200, host a show during the third three-day weekend of August with threshing, logging and sawmill demonstrations. Their historic village, established in 1976, preserves historic buildings that have been moved in from the area, the oldest being the Osage Baptist Church from 1887.

DRIVING TOUR

WILDERNESS DRIVE

Wilderness Drive

Wilderness Drive, a favorite scenic route for motorists and bicyclists, leads west from the Mary Gibbs Mississippi Headwaters Center at the Headwaters and loops around the interior of the park to the Jacob V. Brower Visitor Center. Bike and drive with caution, as summer weekends bring heavier auto and motorcycle traffic, and everyone has to share the road. The contrast between logged and untouched areas along the first stretch of Wilderness Drive is less striking now than it was during its first year, 1925, when timber companies had cut most of the big pines in this area. Now the "young" red pines are 80–100 years old, and mature large-toothed aspen provide the last splash of yellow-orange in late fall. After you drive by Bert's Cabins you will find the gravel road to Lake Ozawindib boat landing and fishing pier straight ahead. Turn south (left), where the drive follows the old park boundary. All the land to your right was clear-cut before lumber interests donated or sold it to the park in 1919, pushing the boundary line 2 miles farther west. The road to Lake Ozawindib Group Center heads right as the road narrows.

Where the one-way road begins, the forest on your left holds old-growth pines and hardwoods, while the right side consists of mostly 100-year-old aspen and sugar maple. The Merschman Thompson Snowmobile Trail (a possible future bike trail connecting to the Headwaters) meets the drive here. Just before you reach the Wilderness Sanctuary, there is a small parking lot and information station on your left, serving the Blowdown and Landmark Trails. Landmark Trail gives a great introduction to the Itasca Wilderness Sanctuary Scientific and Natural Area and National Natural Landmark, which protect a total of

DRIVING TOUR

2,000 acres. Across the road, Blowdown Trail highlights an area of aspen re-growth after a storm in 1995. The next parking area serves the half-mile Bohall Trail, the only trail that enters the Wilderness Sanctuary. The next lot serves the CCC Forestry Demo Trail on the west side of Wilderness Drive. Take the short walk for a look at red pines that were planted in the 1930s, so you can see how they compare to 300-year-old monarchs across the road.

When you reach Two Spot Trail, Wilderness Drive turns left at the site of the old Middlewest forestry cabin, which has crumbled and disappeared, marked now by a sign and a hole in the ground. This eastward section of the drive is hilly and winds through beautiful groves of maple and red pine. A fun, vigorous workout for bicyclists, even experienced riders should use caution while flying down these long, steep hills. The drive passes by Large White Pine Trail, which has a few parking spaces. The next lot serves Large Red Pine Trail and the Bison Kill Site (see Indigenous People, page 195) and has a scenic view of Nicollet Creek up and down the valley. The parking area for Nicollet Trail is a short distance beyond, followed by the turn to Elk Lake Group Camp.

The drive meets Elk Lake in a sunny spot with a boat landing and gravel beach. From Elk Lake it climbs back up to the DeSoto Trailhead and then reaches the parking lot for Aiton Heights Fire Tower. If you plan to park here and take the 0.5-mile walk uphill to the tower, remember that you are on a one-way road, so don't miss the turnoff, which is about 9 miles from Mary Gibbs Mississippi Headwaters Center.

Wilderness Drive continues past Deer Park and Ozawindib Trails but has no parking, as those trails begin at the Douglas Lodge area. Bikers must slow down on the long drop from Deer Park Trail, past Ozawindib Trail, and around the left-hand curve at Mary Lake, if you don't want to follow others before you who have missed the turn and plow into the cattails on Mary's north shore. When you reach the Mary Lake boat landing, the road returns to two-way traffic and leads back past the East Entrance cabin to Douglas Lodge Road and Main Park Drive near the Jacob V. Brower Visitor Center. A complete loop around Wilderness Drive and Main Park Drive is 16 miles.

LA SALLE LAKE STATE RECREATION AREA (SRA) LOOP (36 MILES)

La Salle Lake SRA

From the North Entrance at MN-200, go 6.3 miles north on Clearwater County 2, then turn right (east) on Clearwater County 40 (230th Street) which turns into Hubbard County 9, for 3.3 miles. You will find a parking area for the Scientific & Natural Area on your left near an open field, and the main SRA entrance beyond the LaSalle Creek bridge, on your right. Continue to Becida and turn right on Hubbard County 3 until you reach US-71/MN-200. Turn right (west) to return to the East Entrance in 2 miles.

PARK RAPIDS VIA US-71 (20 MILES)

From the Jacob V. Brower Visitor Center, go to the East Entrance, taking a right on MN-200 and right on US-71 south. Or, except in winter, you can follow the South Entrance Road and turn right on US-71 south. You can also reach Park Rapids via Lake George and Emmaville on Hubbard County 4, with an optional detour to Dorset, 3 miles farther east via Hubbard County 18.

Blackberries

Josephine Lake, Sumacs

156

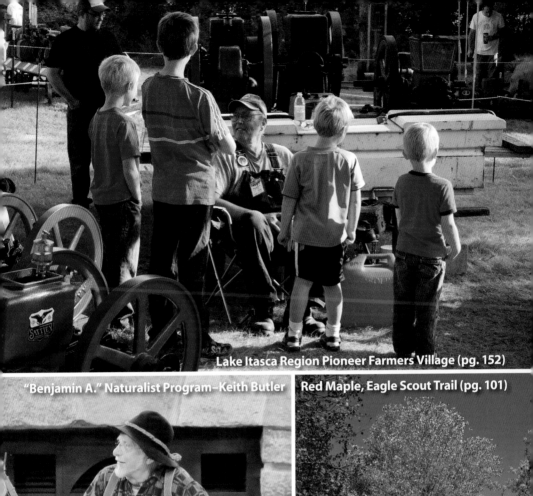
Lake Itasca Region Pioneer Farmers Village (pg. 152)

"Benjamin A." Naturalist Program–Keith Butler

Red Maple, Eagle Scout Trail (pg. 101)

Closed Gentian

Common Loon

Jefferson Highway Marker (pg. 231)

Bike Trail, Picnic Grounds

British Soldier Lichen, Dr. Roberts Trail (pg. 86)

Eagle Scout Trail, Lind Saddle Marker (pg. 101)

Douglas Lodge Cabin

Northern Crescent Butterfly

Red Pine Trail (pg. 121)

RED PINE TRAIL

Mushrooms on Stump

Lovelis Lake Marker, MN-113

CIVILIAN CONSERVATION CORPS
LOVELIS LAKE CAMP 1933-1941

Douglas Lodge

Dr. Roberts Trail [Courtesy of Trista Little] (pg. 86)

Fishing Pier and Coborn's Cruises, Lake Itasca

Ozawindib Trail (pg. 117)

NCT near Morrison Lake (pg. 108)

NCT DeSoto Backcountry Campsite (pg. 108)

Skijoring [Courtesy of Paul Peterson]

Landmark Interpretive Trail (pg. 93)

Headwaters Signpost

HERE 1475 FT
ABOVE
THE OCEAN
THE MIGHTY
MISSISSIPPI
BEGINS
TO FLOW
ON ITS
WINDING WAY
2552 MILES
TO THE
GULF OF
MEXICO

Okerson Heights Trail (pg. 119)

Wilderness Drive

Mississippi Headwaters

Pioneer Cemetery

Wilderness Drive Ski Trail

Wilderness Drive

NCT near Morrison Lake (pg. 108)

Preacher's Grove

Dogsledding

CCC Forestry Demonstration Trail (pg. 78)

Old Timer's Cabin

OLD TIMERS
CABIN

Aiton Heights Fire Tower (pg. 66)

Big Red Pine Trail (pg. 70)

Red Pine Trail (pg. 121)

Whipple Lake, Nicollet Trail (pg. 103)

LaSalle Valley, Beaver Trail (pg. 68)

WHIPPLE
LAKE

Old Timer's Cabin

Hernando DeSoto Lake, Tamaracks

Preacher's Grove

Historic Lake Itasca Post Office

Schoolcraft Marker, near
Douglas Lodge

ITASCA LAKE
SOURCE OF THE MISSISSIPPI PROVED
DISCOVERED BY
HENRY R SCHOOLCRAFT
FROM THE
SUMMIT OF THIS HILL
JULY 13 1832

Iron Corner Backcountry Campsite

Backcountry Camping at Itasca

Get away from it all at a backcountry campsite at Itasca.

In addition to the large drive-in campgrounds, Itasca State Park and the North Country Trail offer the quiet option of backcountry campsites for those willing to carry a backpack and do a little hiking.

DeSoto Backcountry Campsite

Here is a description of each backcountry site to help you pick exactly the right site for your visit. Most of these sites can be reserved, so check for availability in advance of your visit.

B01 and **B02** (see page 103) are located on the shore of Whipple Lake, 2.3 miles along the Nicollet Trail. Here you'll find scenic pines and a tree for ax-throwing practice!

B03 and **B04** (see page 101) overlook Brower Island on Hernando DeSoto Lake on the North Country Trail, about 0.25 mile west of the Nicollet/Eagle Scout Trail junction. Each has steps down to the lake and a swimmable shoreline.

B05 (see page 79) lies on the southeastern corner of McKay Lake and is found amid the shelter of white pines. It is 2.7 miles from Douglas Lodge on Deer Park Trail.

B06 (see page 101) is located on Iron Corner Lake on the east end of Eagle Scout Trail and within 1.5 miles of the South Entrance parking lot via the North Country Trail. A huge white pine shelters this campsite, set near the junction of Hubbard, Clearwater and Becker Counties.

B07, **B08** and **B09** are clustered together on the Myrtle Lake crossover between Deer Park and Ozawindib Trails. You could reach these sites from Red Pine Trail (see page 121) off the South Entrance Road or Deer Park Trail (see page 79) or Ozawindib Trail (see page 117) from Douglas Lodge. All of these routes are just under 2 miles. The first site above the shore has an open area with light tree cover, and the two sites on a peninsula are sunny and brushy, with small pines and birch.

B10 and **B11** (see page 79) are both sheltered by red pines on Deer Park Lake and Deer Park Trail. Deer Park Camp, B10, is on the south end of the lake just beyond the Ozawindib/Myrtle Crossover (see page 117), about 1.5 miles from Douglas Lodge. Coffee Break Camp, B11, is out on a point on the lake and is just over a mile from Douglas Lodge.

The Laurentian Lakes Chapter of the NCT maintains a campsite that is within the Itasca State Park boundary, located 2 miles east of Anchor Matson Road, or just over 3 miles west of the Morrison Lake access lot off MN-113. This first-come, first-served site sits above the shore of a small lake and has a fire ring, log benches and a primitive pit toilet.

Deer Park Backcountry Campsite

Showy Lady's Slipper

Natural History

Although the plants and animals of Itasca State Park could fill several guide books, here is a brief summary of the natural history of the region and just a few of the plants and animals that make it a special place.

With its wide variety of forest types, old and new alike, Itasca has a rich diversity of wildflowers, birds and animals that you may not easily find in other habitats. As you see plants and animals around that are new to you, look them up in a field guide. Then consider how they fit into the particular forest community where you have found them.

Jewelweed and Cattails

Elk Lake

Natural History

Located amid an ever-changing intersection of prairie, hardwoods, conifers and wetlands, Itasca State Park is home to an incredible variety of plants, mammals and birds. Consider this a modest introduction to what you might see as you explore the park.

THE GLACIERS SET THE STAGE

At the peak of the most recent glacial period, which began about 75,000 years ago, Itasca State Park was covered in a sheet of ice thousands of feet thick. Over thousands of years this glacier advanced and retreated several times, relentlessly dragging and depositing a mix of sand, gravel, rock and clay—"glacial till"—over most of the state. The Itasca area was affected by what is now called the Wadena Lobe of the glacier, which brought material from as far away as Hudson Bay and stagnated around Itasca for several hundred years, advancing and melting at about the same rate. The deposits piled up 600 feet deep along the broad shelf of the Itasca Moraine, which extends east and west of Itasca for miles.

BUILDING ITASCA, FEATURE BY FEATURE

The moving ice piled the glacial till into knobs (hills) and kettles (depressions and lakes) between hills and ridges. Sometimes water collected under the glacier, melting from the warmth of the ground beneath it. Water could build up to the point that it would belch out all at once, carrying great loads of sediment that spilled out over a broad outwash plain. This flushing happened repeatedly, scouring out tunnel valleys as deep as 200 feet or more through the Lake Itasca area, and led to the creation of the valley south of Mary Lake and LaSalle Creek that leads northward through LaSalle Lake. Rivers flowing under the ice deposited material that built up over time. When the ice melted, this left winding ridges called eskers. One example of this is Schoolcraft Hill above Douglas Lodge. Another esker crosses East Entrance Road near its midpoint. As the glacier finally receded for good around 12,000 years ago, it left behind ice blocks in some of the kettles and tunnel valleys, which later melted to form the lakes now sprinkled throughout the landscape. There are around 150 lakes of two acres or more in Itasca State Park alone, and the area is strewn with peat bogs and marshes.

A CHANGING FOREST

From pollen studies in the bogs that the glaciers left behind, we know that a boreal forest of spruce and aspen was the first to cover the barren ground. Jack pine and red pine emerged and thrived until about 8,500 years ago, but as the climate continued to get warmer, an oak savanna of prairie grasses and more-widely spaced trees took over. Archaic Indian bands were active here during this period, as shown by the Bison Kill Site (see page 195). A cooling climate and increased moisture 2,700 years ago stimulated the growth of white pine forests. The jack pine and red pine returned about 1,000 years ago, and all three pines, along with a mixed forest of other conifers and deciduous trees, have been abundant through the present day. These plant communities (biomes) are referred to as the Pine Moraines and Outwash Plains subsections of the Northern Coniferous Forest.

THE FORESTS TODAY

Itasca's forests feature many hardwoods and conifers; white, red and jack pine are distributed throughout the park and form uniform stands after a fire or

179

other major disturbances. Several red pine stands, like Preacher's Grove, can be traced back to a fire in 1714. White and red pines are known to live for over 400 years. Jack pine is common in the park as well. Its pine cones are smaller and usually tightly closed; they open best after a fire, so jack pines develop in dense stands after a burn. Although they are usually harvested in Minnesota at age 60–80, one jack pine in the Boundary Waters Canoe Area was over 240 years old. Balsam fir, which favors moister areas, has soft, aromatic needles, and snowshoe hares and other small mammals and birds rely on dense stands of balsam for shelter. White spruce, with its prickly needles and scaly bark, can grow quite large and tolerates drier soils than black spruce, which is often found with tamarack in bogs. Indians used the roots and pitch from black spruce to seal their birchbark canoes. Northern white cedar likes less acidic lowlands. All conifers have evergreen needles except the tamarack, which sheds its needles in the winter after turning to a soft gold in late fall.

A NEW FOREST FILLS IN

After timber companies rolled in and logged some of the native pine forest in the early 1900s, aspen, birch, maples and oaks tended to take over those areas. The softer and fast-growing balsam poplar, large-toothed aspen and quaking aspen can all reproduce with seedlings but are more likely to spread by suckering from the roots, so a single tree can spread to cover an acre or more once light is available to new shoots. Known for forming huge clones over time, a stand of quaking aspen can consist of a few multi-stemmed massive plants with widely spread root systems and may quickly carpet a clear-cut logged area at the expense of pines and other species. Sugar maples reproduce by spawning thousands of seedlings, which produce an autumn understory of yellow leaves. The flash of red maple is easy to spot in the fall around lakes and wetlands. American basswood, a fast-growing tree often associated with maple stands, has soft, white wood that is prized by carvers. Basswood saplings have huge, heart-shaped leaves, and clumps of younger stems often surround the main trunk. The graceful white clumps of paper birch are seen throughout all forest types in Itasca.

A changing climate could bring more changes to Itasca's forests in the future, with warmer temperatures generally favoring trees like white pine and bur oak over red and jack pines, spruce and fir. Without the prolonged extreme winter cold spells that have held bark beetles and budworms in check in the past, more trees of all types will be vulnerable to infestation.

ITASCA'S ICONIC ANIMALS

Moose, elk, bison and woodland caribou once roamed the pre-settlement forest in what is now Itasca State Park, along with an occasional grizzly bear. There are no longer any grizzly bears in the region, and there haven't been any reports of one since 1881, when North-Wind, an American Indian from Pine Point, claimed that he killed an "immense" bear with a "grizzly grey" coat a few miles south of Lake Itasca. He said that "she was as large as an ordinary cow, and would weigh at least 700 pounds." Sometimes brown or cinnamon-colored, the black bear is now Minnesota's only bear. Weighing several hundred pounds, this omnivore eats nuts, berries, plants, fish, small mammals and carrion. In the spring and summer, bears tear logs to pieces in search of their favorite delicacy, ant pupae. Summer finds them in blueberry and blackberry patches. Bears hibernate in a den, typically under a fallen tree, during the winter months. Their cubs are born during this time and nursed by their sleeping mother until spring. All bears, especially mother bears and their cubs, should definitely be left alone. Attacks on people are uncommon, but this is one animal that should not be fed, provoked or approached.

Mary Lake Deer Exclosure

DEER, ELK AND MOOSE

The Park Rapids Enterprise reported in 1930 that a group of hikers encountered eight deer and ten elk, but today the elk are long gone, and the last moose in the area was spotted in the mid-1990s. Nonetheless, whitetail deer are everywhere, and visitors enjoy seeing them feeding on roadsides in the mornings and evenings. In the 1930s, gray wolves had been exterminated, and deer were protected from hunting within Itasca State Park; they became so numerous that they consumed all of the young pine trees, preventing pine regeneration. The Mary Lake Deer Exclosure (see page 98) was built to protect some of the trees and provides a vivid picture of just how widespread the problem was. Because of the incredible deer population density, deer numbers went through cycles of booms and then crashes, which often ended in widespread starvation in winter. In a severe winter, up to 2,000 animals could perish. After attempts to relocate and feed the deer failed, deer hunting within the park finally resumed in 1945. The annual November hunt and the return of the gray wolf have helped to keep their numbers in check. (Visitors to the park during the first week of November would be wise to wear blaze orange.)

Gray Wolf

THE RETURN OF THE GRAY WOLF

Rarely seen but nearly always present somewhere in the park, the gray wolf (timber wolf) has rebounded from near-extinction, thanks to the protection of the Endangered Species Act. In recent years, a pack or two has been roaming through the backcountry area of the park. Since losing its endangered status in 2012, the wolf is once again a limited target for hunters and trappers, although it remains protected within Itasca's boundaries.

Raccoon

NIGHTTIME BANDITS

Though encounters with large animals are uncommon in Itasca State Park, you should still take care to secure your food, whether you are in a large campground or at a backcountry camp. Raccoons are the usual nighttime "companions," and they roam about in search of picnic lunches and scraps. On one of our first family camping trips, we pitched our tent on a "raccoon highway" and faced a long night of shuffling, barking and growling, with a nearby light creating an endless stream of raccoon silhouettes on our tent walls. These famous opportunists will eat anything and prefer to live near water. Although they may act tame, they should be respected as powerful, compact predators, and they are best avoided.

Beaver

A THRIVING BEAVER POPULATION

Another denizen of swamps and lakes, the beaver was nearly wiped out in northern Minnesota during the fur trade of the 1700s and 1800s. They were reintroduced into the park in the early 1900s, and there are now 600–1000 individual animals in Itasca. Their lodges of sticks and mud are present on most of the open-water wetlands and lakes in the park, and the hillsides around their homes are cleaned out of aspen, willows and alders, their preferred foods. Beaver dams, marvels of engineering, raise water levels in a pond or stream valley, permitting the beaver year-round access to the underwater entrance of their house and encouraging willow and alder growth in the shallows. The ponds benefit ducks, frogs and other species. Muskrats also live around lakes and wetlands but build grass houses, not dams.

TINY MAMMALS

The tiniest mammals in the park, including mice and voles, are everywhere, though they live under the leaves, so you are more likely to spot their tracks in the snow than actually see them. You may also find weasel tracks, as they pursue rodents through their surface runways. Other common foragers in the weasel family are minks, northern river otters and fishers.

BATS

Little Brown Bat

If you see a bat flapping around at night, it is most likely a little brown bat, a tiny, winged mammal that roosts in attics or trees during the summer and caves or mines in the winter. Most bats spend their days in trees or other natural hideouts, but during the night they eat up to half their body weight in insects. Although bats are known to occasionally carry rabies, their impact on insect populations benefits campers as well as farmers.

BIRDS

Trumpeter Swans

You don't need fancy binoculars and an encyclopedic life list of sightings to appreciate the birds of Itasca State Park. Itasca is special for both novice and experienced birders because it is home to many habitat types and a variety of bird species. Over 200 species nest here, including bald eagles and trumpeter swans, both of which were once endangered but are now common sights. Children are fascinated by birds and will enjoy the hummingbirds, chickadees and nuthatches that visit the feeders at the Jacob V. Brower Visitor Center. Because most old-growth forests were logged long ago, the birds and animals that rely on them are in serious decline. Thankfully, Itasca is a sanctuary for species like the red crossbill and northern goshawk that depend on wide expanses of mature forest.

Common Loon

WATERFOWL

Lake Itasca and many of the smaller lakes hold numerous water-fowl, such as ducks, geese, ospreys, and gulls, as well as great blue herons, sandpipers and other shorebirds. The call of the loon is heard on quiet summer evenings throughout the park, and red-winged blackbirds are common in the cattails and wetlands. Pairs of trumpeter swans, which have made a great comeback in recent years, are often seen on smaller lakes and wetlands, including those along US-71 south of the park.

Black-backed Woodpecker

SOME RARE PARK DENIZENS

In addition to the more common pileated and hairy woodpeckers, the park's forests are home to the rarer black-backed woodpecker and a host of sought-after songbirds, including scarlet tanagers, indigo buntings, golden-crowned kinglets, various sparrows and wrens and more than 20 species of warblers. Predators, such as goshawks and owls, also thrive in the wide areas of undisturbed forest, and populations of smaller hawks and falcons, such as the merlin, are rebounding. Experienced birders will be drawn by rarer birds, such as the red crossbill, which is found around the mature red pines near Douglas Lodge and other areas. Boggy areas, including the nearby Lake Alice Bog, hold Connecticut and golden-winged warblers and olive-sided, yellow-bellied and alder flycatchers.

Ctenuchid Moth, Pearly Everlasting

BUTTERFLIES, MOTHS AND DRAGONFLIES

Itasca participates in an annual butterfly count in mid-July, which celebrates the "flying flowers" that visit the abundant wildflowers of the park on sunny summer days. Over 60 species have been spotted in the park in recent years, including the milkweed-loving monarch butterfly, whose numbers have dwindled because of bad winter weather during migration coupled with a reduction of its favorite food source due to herbicide use and habitat loss. Overall the north woods harbor up to 125 species of butterflies and even more moths, which are more active at night.

Dragonflies and damselflies not only do their share of damage to the mosquito and fly populations, but they also are forage for insect-eating birds. Dragonfly larvae live in the shallows of lakes and ponds and are a favorite food of bass and other fish. The various species of dragonflies hatch at different times during the summer, and you may see several varieties in the air all at once.

Wood Frog

FROGS, TOADS AND SALAMANDERS

Amphibians, such as frogs and toads, also feast on aquatic insects and are active throughout the summer. Spring peepers and chorus frogs are the first to chime in during spring. Well-camouflaged wood frogs quack softly, like a flock of feeding mallards. Leopard frogs are also active in April and May in wet, grassy meadows. Mink frogs begin their "cut-cut-cut" chorus, like horses' hooves, in June, about the time American toads move from wetlands to higher ground for the summer. Blue-spotted and tiger salamanders live around ponds and moist woods but are hard to see, as they spend most of their time moving around under leaves and woody debris.

Snapping Turtle

SNAKES, SKINKS AND TURTLES

You may see the occasional garter snake or redbelly snake, but there are no rattlesnakes or other venomous species in this part of Minnesota. The secretive prairie skink, the only common lizard here, is the master of cutting its losses. It can lose its tail to a predator and escape to regrow a replacement. Walk by a pond or lakeshore on a sunny day, and painted turtles will be sunning themselves on rocks or logs. The snapping turtle, Minnesota's largest, lives for decades and may grow as large as 20" in length, weighing up to 65 pounds. Females lumber out of the water in June and search for sandy spots to lay their eggs. If you see one, don't approach it, as they can lunge quickly with their powerful neck and jaws.

Asters, Brower Trail

WILDFLOWERS

Itasca features a variety of plant communities, so it's no surprise that it has an array of wildflowers. Undisturbed areas in the pines and moist forests sport lady's slippers, while bogs and inaccessible areas hide rarer orchids and other endangered plants. Well-traveled areas of the park have a mix of native flowers and European invaders. As you marvel at them, remember that the flowers are there for everyone to enjoy and are not to be picked or dug up. It can take 17 years for a lady's slipper to bloom from a seedling, and they are dependent on soil conditions and symbiotic fungi, which makes them very difficult to transplant.

SPRING ARRIVALS

In addition to the popular lady's slippers, there are many other flowers that show up in spring, beginning with white bloodroot, white and purple hepatica, yellow and blue violets and the tiny, white wood anemone. Marsh marigolds fill the bog area on Dr. Roberts Trail in May, and the droopy yellow bells of large-flowered bellwort are common throughout the upland forest. Summer brings roadside displays of black-eyed Susans, northern bedstraw and hare bells, among others.

Yellow Lady's Slipper

FLOWERS FOR ALL SEASONS

In midsummer, the marshy area below Douglas Lodge lights up with orange trumpets of jewelweed and the magenta blooms of swamp milkweed and Joe-pye weed, followed by the delicate flowers of wild rice in midsummer and then asters and goldenrod in the fall. Itasca has up to 18 different asters, and if you look closely you may see a half-dozen species growing in the same area. Closed gentian can be found a short distance beyond on the Brower Trail.

Lake Itasca, Trumpeter Swans

MUCH MORE TO EXPLORE

Of course, this is just a sampling of the wildlife to see at Itasca State Park; for a more in-depth look, bring along a few field guides (see page 258 for my recommendations) and enjoy the many flowers, birds and wildlife that abound here; the experience is sure to leave you richer and wiser.

Red Squirrel

Preacher's Grove Fog

ITASCA
history

Itasca History

Itasca's story is intertwined with human history. This section covers the history of the Itasca region, from its first inhabitants to the present day.

One of the wonderful things about Itasca is the way that archaeology has uncovered its past, with some finds dating back thousands of years. Learning how people lived then and how everything changed once the European explorers and settlers moved in gives one a better understanding and appreciation for the park as it is today. This section also covers Jacob V. Brower's fight to establish Itasca State Park and its development in the twentieth century.

"At the Source of the Father of Waters" Pageant Photo

Bison at Itasca

Indigenous People of the Itasca State Park Region

Try to imagine Itasca as it might have looked just as the last of the glacial ice receded 11,000 years ago: The tundra left behind is filling in with a forest of spruce and fir, and the last of the giant bison, 25 percent larger than today's plains buffalo, graze the prairie, followed by bands of Paleo-Indian hunters. While the only solid local evidence of the presence of Paleo-Indians is one projectile point found at the Pamida construction site in Bemidji, we know they roamed the area, living on game and whatever nuts, berries and other edible foods were available. Creation stories of the Anishinaabe (which means "the original people" and refers to the group known as the Ojibwe or the Chippewa) tell of Kitchi Manido, the Great Spirit, dreaming of the beauty of the earth and creating the four elements of rock, water, fire and wind. Their stories tell how he breathed life of a different character into each, and then created the earth with everything in it, including humans, to whom he gave the power to dream. Other stories tell of a great flood destroying everything but the birds and animals, stranding Naanabozho, the good spirit (or the woodland trickster in some forms of the story), in his canoe with the animals. He attempts to retrieve land from the water by directing the animals to dive down for it, but only the humble muskrat finally succeeds. With no written record before the eighteenth century, their stories convey the sense that the Anishinaabe have always been here.

THE BISON KILL SITE

In 1937, as road crews were rebuilding a bridge over Nicollet Creek on Wilderness Drive, they uncovered many large animal bones in addition to those of fish, birds and other smaller mammals. Further study then and during extensive excavations in 1964–1965 showed that two-thirds of the bones were most likely *Bison occidentalis*, a species of giant bison that became extinct 5,000 years ago. This species of giant bison may have evolved into today's smaller North American bison (*Bison bison*). The remains found on the Bison Kill Site, as well as stone tools and spear points, suggest a date of 7,000–8,000 years before the present. The climate then was at its maximum warmth after the glacial age, and what is now Itasca was on the edge of the prairie. There were no real signs of habitation, so it is likely that these eastern Archaic hunters, who lived from 8,000 to 3,000 years ago, used this site primarily for hunting bison, which could get mired down in the muddy streambed in the fall and be easier to kill.

Jacob V. Brower

RELICS FROM THE ELK LAKE CULTURE

Another chapter in Itasca's history is being revealed now, as shovel tests in a proposed boat launch ramp near LaSalle Creek in the La Salle Lake State Recreation Area have been found to contain pottery sherds dating back to 3,180 years ago. The "Brainerd Ware" shards are artifacts from the Elk Lake Culture, one of the Early Woodland Indian cultures. The Itasca Indian Cemetery and mounds, located north of the picnic grounds, date back to the Late Woodland Indian culture of 500 to 900 years ago. First excavated by Jacob V. Brower, the mounds were related to a large Woodland village on the northeast shore of Lake Itasca, extending well south of the Headwaters. Nine of the ten mounds were excavated by Brower in 1895 and rebuilt in 1898, and all indicated burial sites. Up to 100,000 mounds may have been built from the Ohio Valley to the Upper Mississippi Valley, with many sites in Minnesota and Wisconsin. The Woodland Indians were the first in northern Minnesota to use pottery, and other sites have shown evidence of wild rice use from over 1,800 years ago. Another Woodland site over 500 years old is located on Chambers Creek near the Elk Lake boat landing.

THE SANTEE DAKOTA

The Santee Dakota (sometimes referred to as Sioux, after the French term *Nadouessioux*) inhabited northern Minnesota prior to the Ojibwe, and evidence of their villages has been found throughout the area, including at the Woodland Indian village site on Lake Itasca. Unlike the Lakota, one group of the Dakota Seven Council Fires who inhabited the plains, the woodland Dakota lived on fish, game and other seasonal foods. Like the Ojibwe that followed, they also relied on wild rice, berries, nuts, roots and maple syrup, living and moving in harmony with the land. For generations the Dakota were relatively untouched by conflict with others and, because of their isolation, initially avoided the diseases brought by Europeans, such as smallpox and measles, which had decimated eastern tribes.

FIREARMS AND CONFLICT

The stage was set for change in 1639 when the Iroquois of Pennsylvania and New York obtained firearms from the Dutch. With English support, the unified Iroquois attacked the French, and their friends, the Algonquian-speaking tribes, and began driving the Ojibwe and others west. For many years the Ojibwe, often accompanied by French fur traders, lived peacefully near the Dakota and intermarried and traded with them. But a series of events and conflicts in the 1730s led to frequent battles and a cycle of violence that lasted beyond the 1825 Treaty of Prairie du Chien, when the U.S. government negotiated a peace that defined tribal boundaries and left the Ojibwe in control of northern Minnesota.

FAMOUS EXPLORERS MEET THE OJIBWE

In the Headwaters region, the Ojibwe hunted and gathered wild rice and other wild foods, just as the woodland Dakota had before them. Ojibwe guides from the Pillager band based at Cass Lake and Leech Lake led early explorers Henry Rowe Schoolcraft and Joseph Nicollet to Lake Itasca in the 1830s. There were no Ojibwe villages in the immediate Itasca area at the time, and they followed routes known only to those who regularly hunted there.

EUROPEANS ENCROACH

When European settlers gradually encroached on the Ojibwe's territory, it affected food production in the area and led to fewer furs being harvested, destroying the Ojibwe economy. Soon after, the Ojibwe were forced into a series of treaties from 1837 through 1867, essentially trading their land for food and other goods. In the Treaty of 1855, the Ojibwe ceded much of northern Minnesota, including the Headwaters. The treaty was negotiated primarily by Aish-ke-vo-go-zhe (Flat Mouth), an important member of the Pillager band of Chippewa.

INDIAN REMOVAL AND RESERVATIONS

Following the removal of the Ojibwe and Dakota to reservations, the door was opened to white settlers. White Earth Indian Reservation, which borders Itasca State Park to the west, was established in 1867. Initially populated by Ojibwe removed from Mille Lacs, they were later joined by other bands. When the Nelson Act of 1889 allowed the sale of allotted tribal land to nonnatives, much of the reservation land and timber were improperly sold or seized, and tribal members now own only about 10 percent of the land within the reservation. Tribal leaders and agencies like the White Earth Land Recovery Project are working to recover more land for the tribe.

Father Louis Hennepin

Early Mississippi Explorers: De Soto, La Salle, Hennepin, Du Luth, Pike, Cass, Beltrami

"The mystery of a river's source is not to be taken lightly. What is it that has driven man to hazard life and fortune tracing the paths of the world's greatest rivers back to their humblest beginnings?"
—Steven P. Hall

THE EUROPEAN SEARCH FOR THE HEADWATERS BEGINS

Beginning with Alonso Álvarez de Pineda, who claimed to have sailed up
the lower Mississippi River in 1519 but more likely just reached Mobile Bay,
and Hernando de Soto, who crossed the Mississippi in 1541, generations of
European explorers led expeditions farther and farther up the river, fascinated
with the search for its source. René-Robert Cavelier, Sieur de La Salle, who
had claimed the Mississippi basin for France, led a group of French explorers
down the Illinois River in 1680.

FATHER HENNEPIN MEETS THE DAKOTA

Upon reaching the Mississippi, La Salle dispatched voyageur Michel Accault
(Ako) with explorer Antoine Auguelle Picard du Gay and Father Louis
Hennepin, clad in his hooded robe and sandals, to explore farther up the
uncharted Mississippi. Leaving on March 8, they battled icy waters and
extreme conditions and hardships until, on April 11, still well south of Lake
Pepin, they encountered a band of 120 Dakota Indians heading south with the
intent of attacking the Miamis. Though neither spoke a word of each other's
language, the explorers were able to convey to the Dakota that their enemies
had departed, and so the disappointed band returned to their Mille Lacs
villages with the three Frenchmen in tow. From the moment of their first
"capture," the three often felt their lives to be in grave danger, but their
unfamiliarity with Dakota language and customs left them with no idea of
their captors' intent. Exhausted and unable to keep up with the relentless
speed of the journey, Father Hennepin required constant assistance, even
claiming that the Indians would light grass fires behind him and then rush
him along to keep up to their torrid pace.

AN ADOPTED FAMILY

On their arrival at Mille Lacs, each of the three was adopted by a separate village. They settled into village life during their two months there and even joined the entire band in a buffalo hunt. They were later allowed to leave to meet other explorers from Wisconsin for supplies, and while camped near the St. Croix River, they encountered Daniel Greysolon, Sieur Du Luth, who had come looking for them. His exaggerated claims of a dramatic rescue to the contrary, they were freely traveling on their own then and went back to Mille Lacs with Du Luth for a time before returning down the Mississippi.

THE SOUTHERN REACHES OF THE MISSISSIPPI EXPLORED

Two years later, La Salle and Henri de Tonti (Tonty) left Fort Michilimacinac, Michigan, and traveling via Lake Michigan and the Chicago and Illinois Rivers, reached the Mississippi River and set out to explore the river to its mouth. La Salle left Tonti in Arkansas, and upon reaching present day New Orleans, planted the French flag, claiming the Mississippi drainage for his home country. He left for France, later returned and resumed his explorations but was killed by his own mutinous men in 1687. Tonti, who was unaware of La Salle's demise and searched for him in vain, lived out his life on the lower Mississippi until he died of yellow fever in 1704.

IN SEARCH OF THE HEADWATERS

Lt. Zebulon Pike led an expedition toward the Headwaters in 1805, concluding that Red Cedar Lake (Cass Lake) was the source. Lewis Cass, accompanied by his geologist Henry Rowe Schoolcraft, reached the north shore of that same lake in 1820, again declaring it to be the source of the Mississippi. Giacomo Beltrami, an Italian who added some flamboyance to the area's history, was described by Jacob Brower as a "hero-worshiper, with but one hero, and that himself." Traveling with Maj. Stephen Long's 1823 party up the Red River of the North to Pembina, Beltrami clashed with Long after he sold Long's horse. Beltrami then turned back southeast in search of the Mississippi's source with a Metis guide and two Ojibwe guides. Abandoned by his guides after a Dakota attack, Beltrami found another guide at Red Lake and continued on. As the story goes, he sheltered himself from the rain with a red umbrella throughout the trip. He arrived at a small lake north of Bemidji, which he named Lake Julia after his dear friend Giuliana Spada dei Medici, who had died in Italy in 1820. Perceiving it correctly to be located at a divide between two river drainages, he declared it the source of both the Bloody River (Red River) and the "Julian Source" of the Mississippi, despite the very different conclusions of geographer David Thompson, who had been there 25 years earlier. His guide advised him of the existence of Lac La Biche (Lake Itasca), so he added it to his map as "Doe Lake, W. source of the Mississippi" but never went there.

William Morrison

THE FIRST EUROPEAN TO SEE THE HEADWATERS

William Morrison, a Canadian trader working for Alexander MacKenzie & Co., spent the winter of 1803–1804 at Lac La Folle (Rice Lake), about 10 miles northwest of Itasca in Clearwater County. He traveled to the Headwaters on his way to the post that winter and again in 1811. Although his journals of 20 years were lost when his canoe capsized, he wrote a letter to his brother 50 years later detailing his journeys in the area. Jacob Brower reports that Morrison "freely discussed" his trips to Elk Lake (Lake Itasca) of 1803–1804 and 1811–1812 with his daughter, Mrs. Georgina Demaray, and others in his household. It is likely that he was the first white man to visit the source of the Mississippi.

Henry Rowe Schoolcraft

HENRY ROWE SCHOOLCRAFT

If you walk to the Douglas Lodge cabins and stop by the rock monument at Cabin 7, you will be seeing Lake Itasca from the same viewpoint as Henry Rowe Schoolcraft did in 1832.

However, you will not have just endured a 6-mile portage from Lake Alice, guided by Ozawindib, and hopefully you will not be covered with bug bites and scratches from crashing through the brush and swamps along the way.

A FLUCTUATING BORDER

Why did Schoolcraft make the journey in the first place? Jefferson's Louisiana Purchase of 1803 led to in-depth exploration of the Mississippi River, as a line drawn north from the Mississippi's source to the 49th parallel would define the western boundary of the United States. Although Pike's 1805 claim of Red Cedar Lake (Cass Lake) as the source was clearly incorrect and left the boundary with British territory in doubt, that issue was settled in 1818, when the 49th parallel was accepted as the boundary, extending across Dakota Territory.

SCHOOLCRAFT RETURNS TO THE REGION

Schoolcraft, who had served as geologist and geographer for Lewis Cass on his 1820 expedition to Red Cedar Lake (Cass Lake), was now the Indian agent in charge of the Michigan region based in Sault Ste. Marie. He was invited by Cass, now the U.S. Secretary of War, to travel to Leech Lake to meet with Chippewa chief Aish-ke-vo-go-zhe (Flat Mouth) and other leaders in the region. His charge was to establish U.S. control over the fur trade, vaccinate as many Indians as possible against smallpox, and see what could be done to quiet the conflicts between Ojibwe and Dakota that had once again flared in the region. But his personal goal was to establish the true source of the river, which he referred to as Lac La Biche (Elk Lake). When Schoolcraft arrived, the Ojibwe contacts he made definitively confirmed that this was the Mississippi's source, as they all knew from their hunting expeditions in the region. Its Ojibwe name, *Omashkooz*, refers to the shape of the lake, which resembles an elk's antlers. That name was later transferred to today's Elk Lake, located just south of Lake Itasca's West Arm.

OZAWINDIB, AN INDIAN GUIDE

Schoolcraft's party included William T. Boutwell, Dr. Douglass Houghton, interpreter George Johnston, and a military contingent led by Lt. James Allen. They set out from Sault Ste. Marie on June 7, 1832. At the mouth of the Brule River in Lake Superior they met Ozawindib (Yellow Head), "one of the Principal Chippewas" of the Cass Lake band, who was traveling with his family to Sault Ste. Marie. Ozawindib agreed to turn around to guide Schoolcraft's expedition, and after taking the Savanna Portage west to Sandy Lake, they paddled up the Mississippi River to Cass Lake. The expedition arrived on July 10 to find a flotilla of canoes filled with villagers saluting their arrival at Ozawindib's home. They found an open village in a beautiful setting, high on a hill above the lake, with small fields of corn and potatoes, surrounded by forest. A war party had just returned from a battle with the Dakota, so the visitors witnessed the aftermath of mourning and celebration, capped off by a scalp dance.

THE HEADWATERS FINALLY REACHED

Ozawindib continued to guide Schoolcraft to the Headwaters, as he considered it his family's hunting ground. Favored hunting spots, which might be several days travel from the nearest village, were not necessarily considered to be the exclusive domain of one hunter or one family, as just four years later Nicollet's Pillager guide also claimed Itasca to be his hunting ground. But it makes sense that the same few hunters would repeatedly work a remote area like Itasca, once they had learned the game patterns and seldom-used trails.

Schoolcraft, Allen, Houghton, Johnston and Boutwell went on with a group of Ojibwe, sixteen in all, leaving the tired soldiers behind, as they were concerned that they would be unable to handle the lightweight birchbark canoes required in smaller streams. They paddled upriver to Lac Travers (Lake Bemidji), then turned south, heading up a branch (Schoolcraft River) that led from Kubbakunna Lake, "The Rest in the Path" (Lake Plantagenet). They ascended through the damp, cool forest of pine and tamarack, accompanied "by frequent showers of rain, which gave, as is usual, a peculiar activity and virulence to the musquito." Boutwell, who was particularly annoyed, reported "musketoes by the 10,000 lbs." At the south end of Ossawa Lake (Lake Alice) they waded through a shallow marsh to dry land at a well-used Indian campground, one of several along the portage. Ozawindib led them on a route through a cedar grove, across a swamp of moss-covered fallen trees, and up and down pine-covered ridges of sand and rock. Their excitement at reaching the source grew with each step, until "on turning out of a thicket, into a small weedy opening, the cheering sight of a transparent body of water burst upon our view. It was Itasca Lake— the source of the Mississippi."

Peace Pipe Vista

THE TRUE SOURCE AND AN INVENTED NAME

How did Schoolcraft choose the name, Itasca? Along the way, he asked his colleague Rev. W. T. Boutwell for the Latin for "true source." He gave him *veritas caput*, "truth, head," and Schoolcraft then drew Itasca from the center of those words. Schoolcraft confirmed this in a letter to Dr. Addison Philleo, dated July 25, 1832, and this explanation was published in the newspaper *The Galenian* and others. But later, Schoolcraft denied the name's Latin origins, which remained in doubt until Boutwell himself confirmed the story to Jacob Brower in 1872. Perhaps in an attempt to give the name a romantic Ojibwe association, Schoolcraft wrote in his *Summary Narrative of 1855* that the name came from a poem, the first verse of which read:

Within a beauteous basin, fair outspread
Hesperian woodlands of the western sky,
As if in Indian Myths a truth there could be read
And these were tears indeed, by fair Itasca shed.

He claimed that this was based on an Ojibwe legend that his guide told him. The myth was reputed to tell the story of an Indian maiden, daughter of Nanabozho, who was borne to the underworld by an evil spirit. But the poem and the myth were most likely his own.

A CONTROVERSIAL STAMP OF OWNERSHIP

No one knows why Schoolcraft denied that he had chosen the name from *veritas caput*. Perhaps the Latin seemed too mundane for his lofty ideals, or he wished to endow it with some romantic Indian connotation so that it would be better accepted by the traders, Indians, and others who objected to changing the traditional Ojibwe/French name. A name change is a stamp of ownership, after all. Major Lawrence Taliaferro, Indian agent at Fort Snelling, wrote in 1836, "Oh thou wiper out of names of places – to swell your own consequence upon the fall of La Beasch & rise [of] Ithaka or Itashkah." Even after the name change, some continued to refer to the old name. For example, Joseph Nicollet always referred to Lake Itasca as "Lac la Biche" in the journal of his 1836 expedition.

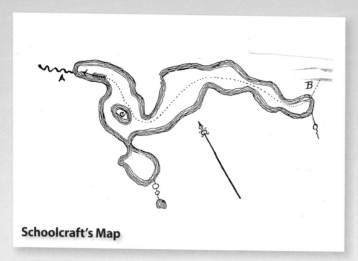

Schoolcraft's Map

A BRIEF TRIP ON THE LAKE

The group paddled from Mary Creek through the lake, stopping at Schoolcraft Island, but they did not explore the West Arm, or today's Nicollet Creek or Elk Lake. This is obvious from Schoolcraft's map, which shows the West Arm to be much shorter than it is. They raised a primitive flag on the island and paddled on to the Headwaters at the north end. Schoolcraft noted the marshy outlet of the Mississippi to be 12 feet wide and over a foot deep. Because the water was cool and clear and had so much more flow than the other streams he had seen, he correctly guessed that the lake was fed by springs. After half a day on the lake, they paddled down the young Mississippi, winding through vast swamps and over rapids, through Lake Traverse (Bemidji) and back to Ozawindib's home on Cass Lake.

A MEETING WITH A PILLAGER CHIEF

From there the explorers headed home, stopping at Leech Lake for a council with the Pillager band, where they were sternly lectured by the respected chief, Aish-ke-vo-go-zhe (Flat Mouth) on the ineffectiveness of treaties in easing their conflict with the Dakota. In a meeting with the expedition, surrounded by his own men, Flat Mouth held up four silver medals that he had been given, now stained with vermillion pigment, and threw them at Schoolcraft's feet. "Take notice," he said, "they are bloody. I wish you to wipe off the blood. I am unable to do it. I find myself irretrievably involved in a war with the Sioux . . . I have heretofore looked for help [from the American government] where we did not find it."

After Dr. Houghton had vaccinated several hundred of the Pillager band against smallpox, Schoolcraft's party portaged to May Lake, then to 11th Crow Wing Lake, descended the Crow Wing River until they met the Mississippi again, and proceeded on to Fort Snelling.

Joseph N. Nicollet

NICOLLET VISITS ITASCA

On Thursday, August 25, 1836, Joseph Nicollet awoke in the Kabekona valley, just two days' journey from Lake Itasca.

He wrote: "This morning for the first time in my life I attended a terrifying concert performed at dawn by wolves whose bands are wont to haunt these totally deserted and virgin forests. It was like a choir of chilling howls that could be heard in the distance on both sides of the river, spreading far and wide across the echoing solitude." The voyageurs listened in awe as the wolves howled across the valley that he described in his 1843 report, whose high banks protected a "thick forest of spruce firs and pines behind and along its banks, and a shrubbery of alders so thickly set that we were obliged to use our hatchets to navigate it." The Kabekona valley, rich in wildlife, "where we saw constantly recurring the footsteps and marks of bears, wolves, deer, and otters," also was filled with "swarms of mosquitoes, that came pouring upon us in torrents, so as, at three different times, to extinguish the lights of my lanterns."

AN EXPLORER WITH A VARIED PAST

Nicollet (referred to as "Jean N. Nicollet" by Brower) had come to explore and map the Upper Mississippi and its sources, following in the footsteps of

Schoolcraft's journey four years before. Born in 1786 in Cluses, France, Joseph Nicolas Nicollet was educated by the Jesuits, preparing him for a career as a gifted mathematician and astronomer. His attempts to apply probability theory to the market began with an initial financial windfall for himself and his friends, but ended in disaster when the market crashed after the French Revolution of 1830. Discredited and ruined, the 44-year-old astronomer sailed to America and soon began work for the Coastal Survey in Washington, D.C. In the fall of 1836, he read Lt. Allen's report of the Schoolcraft expedition to the Mississippi's source and determined that he would embark on his own trip to the area, not only to map and survey the Upper Mississippi to its source, but also to provide a detailed report on the natural history and geography of the region. As he went along, he was fully aware that his explorations would lead to encroaching civilization in his wake. He was fascinated by the Ojibwe people and, like most Europeans of his time, felt that this exposure to Christianity and civilization would be in their best interest.

NICOLLET REACHES LEECH LAKE

Nicollet left Fort Snelling with the support of Indian agent Lawrence Taliaferro and in the company of two French-Americans, Francis Brunia and Desiré, an Ojibwe guide, Chagobay, and Chagobay's ten-year-old son. They traveled to Leech Lake through the rigors of bad weather, weed-choked waterways, and mosquito attacks. Nicollet recorded, "The atmosphere did not treat us like spoiled children." And nearing Leech Lake, he wrote, "We are enduring literally clouds of mosquitoes that rise higher than the tallest trees I could make out towering above the swamps." At Leech Lake, he left Chagobay, now a dear friend, with his family and traveled to Itasca with a new guide, Ke'goue'dgika, the only Pillager present who was familiar with the area.

TRAVELING TO LAKE ITASCA

Following a route through Kabekona Lake and River, Nicollet and his party traveled to Lake Alice and took the 6-mile portage to Lake Itasca, heading for Schoolcraft's vista of four years before. The first mile led through a cedar swamp, then a "hollow filled up with fallen decayed trees . . . and covered with a thick layer of wet moss and other parasites. It is a buried forest, over which another is growing." The men hoisted their loads and trotted through it all, the trot being the standard pace of the voyageur. The speed would allow the canoe carrier to crash through brush and branches without taking the time and energy to push these obstacles aside with his hands.

Nicollet noted: "Brunia, the giant, with the canoe tipped over his head, looking like an enormous seal swimming over shrubbery, opened our path."

MAPPING THE HEADWATERS

Nicollet and his party explored the entire lake and its inlets, using astronomical and barometric observations to map the area. They followed Nicollet Creek, which he considered the "infant Mississippi," to its sources in the springs above Lake Itasca, up through Nicollet Lake and most likely to Whipple Lake, "the very first trickles that will form the Mississippi." They portaged around Chambers Creek, which was completely obstructed with wood and debris, and headed into Elk Lake and explored its tributary streams. After three days on the lake, the group followed the Mississippi River south through Lake Traverse (Bemidji) and back to Fort Snelling. Nicollet's conclusions, which were later published, backed Schoolcraft's assertions that Lake Itasca was indeed the primary source of the Mississippi.

THE CREATION OF THE WHITE EARTH INDIAN RESERVATION

After Schoolcraft and Nicollet had initially mapped the Headwaters region, there were no notable white visitors until the Treaty of 1867 established the White Earth Indian Reservation. Investigative journalist Julius Chambers made a trip representing *The New York Herald* in 1872, after his physician prescribed three months in the open air. He set out with the intent to paddle his canoe, named *Dolly Varden,* from the source of the Mississippi down the entire length of the river. With French-Canadian guide Henry Beaulieu, Ojibwe carrier Ka-ba-be-zen, and a younger, unnamed Ojibwe, they portaged from White Earth to Rice Lake and on to the Mississippi River. After a three-day "struggle with nature," a strenuous tree and boulder-obstructed ascent of the river, the group reached Lake Itasca.

ANOTHER CLAIM TO THE HEADWATERS

Knowing that Schoolcraft had not explored the lake in detail, Chambers' party paddled down the west arm and ascended the creek (Chambers Creek) to Elk Lake. Finding no other significant inlets, Chambers declared Elk Lake to be the true source of the river and renamed it Dolly Varden Lake. He found Nicollet Creek, "The Cradled Hercules," to be "insignificant" when he visited it— perhaps, according to historian Brower, due to the lower water level in 1872 compared to Nicollet's visit in 1836. Chambers went on down the Mississippi, paddling the *Dolly Varden* to within 100 miles of St. Louis, Missouri, in "intolerable heat." Encountering the steamboat *Belle of La Crosse*, "I decided to dodge sunstroke and take her." At St. Louis he transferred to the *James Howard* to complete his journey to New Orleans.

AN ADVENTURE TO REMEMBER

Chambers' adventure provided him with several newspaper articles and inspired his book, *The Mississippi River and its Wonderful Valley*. Though Lake Itasca was ultimately declared the source of the Mississippi and Elk Lake retained its name, Chambers wrote in 1910 that to him, "the Elk Lake trip is a delightful memory, unmarred by a single unfriendly thought."

THE GLAZIER FIASCO

In 1881, Captain Willard Glazier, an adventurer and prolific author, set out to stake his claim to fame at the source of the great river. The grandiose claims that he made after his 1881 expedition may have not stood the test of time, but the name for his expedition—the Glazier Fiasco—did, thanks to a headline penned by Jacob V. Brower in his book, *The Mississippi and its Source*. Leaving from Cleveland, Ohio, with his brother George and reporter Barrett Paine, he traveled through Brainerd, Minnesota, to Leech Lake. With She-na-wi-gi-shick, an Ojibwe guide, the group canoed and portaged to Lake Itasca, arriving at the same vantage point on the east shore as Schoolcraft and Nicollet. Paddling south on the west arm, Glazier's party struggled through the shallow, obstructed water of Chambers Creek to Elk Lake. Nicollet had documented his visit to this lake in 1836, as had Julius Chambers in 1872. But upon his arrival Glazier claimed to be its discoverer, and he immediately named it Lake Glazier. The next morning, the group arose exhausted and hungry, as they'd eaten all of their food, spent their ammunition and lost their fishing tackle. The ill-prepared group left their camp on Schoolcraft Island in desperation and, after less than 24 hours in the area, they headed home.

A PLAGIARIST MAKES HIS CLAIM

When he later found that others had made well-documented visits to Elk Lake before him, Glazier changed his claim to having found that "Lake Glazier" was the "primal reservoir" of the river, rather than Lake Itasca. However, his account of the journey, *Down the Great River*, was filled with plagiarism and inaccuracies. Brower documented nine sections copied from Schoolcraft's accounts, most nearly word for word. Glazier even exactly duplicated a table of weather observations, right down to the last missing number, which had been omitted by Schoolcraft after his thermometer broke.

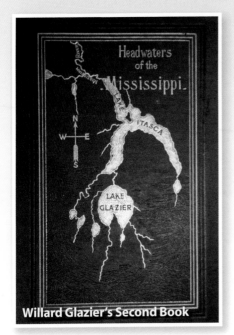

Willard Glazier's Second Book

THE FAKER DOUBLES DOWN

On August 22, 1891, in an attempt to counter years when "spasmodic efforts, partaking for the most part of a disingenuous and personal character, were made by a few cavilers to discredit the author's discovery," Glazier embarked on a second expedition. *Headwaters of the Mississippi*, published in 1893, documents his trip accompanied by a larger and better-organized party. The fifteen travelers included Glazier's daughter Alice and Park Rapids residents Henry J. Cobb, editor of the *Hubbard County Enterprise*, and E. M. Horton and Oliver Storr Keay, both surveyors. They conducted extensive measurements during their nine days in the Headwaters, measuring the tributaries, lake depths and the surface area of Elk Lake, Lake Itasca and the surrounding lakes.

ANOTHER (FALSE) FIRST

Glazier even arranged to have a Mr. Crane perform a worship service and deliver "the first sermon ever preached at the Source of the Mississippi," no doubt to eclipse Rev. Gilfillan's service performed 10 years earlier on the shore of Lake Itasca. All reports are that the party had a fine time, and the trip provided Glazier with numerous photographs and drawings for publication. He delighted in having his daughter Alice along, recalling "that which, perhaps, excited most comment, was the endurance displayed by my daughter, who walked by my side throughout the day, without once complaining of fatigue, a distance of at least twenty miles, although the road was so hilly and rugged in many places as to threaten to precipitate horses and wagons, with their loads, to the bottom of the declivities."

CONSENSUS OVERRULES GLAZIER

However, despite his extensive measurements, illustrations and other documents, Glazier was unable to overcome not only his old reputation and inaccuracies, but also the contradictions of several members who had been along on his expeditions. The consensus remained that Nicollet Creek had twice the flow into Lake Itasca, and that Chambers Creek, the outlet of Elk Lake, was merely another tributary. Willard Glazier's legacy lies in the names of Lake George (for his brother), Lake Alice (in honor of his beloved daughter, although the name is now attached to a different lake nearby, the original now called Hall Lake), Lake Paine (Barrett Paine) and Lake Hattie (from Glazier's map) and their respective townships. He also named the LaSalle River. Keay's instruments and Glazier's book, *Headwaters of the Mississippi*, are on display at the Hubbard County Museum in Park Rapids.

Headwaters

A Scientific Look at the Headwaters

GENERAL JAMES BAKER

General James Baker, U.S. Surveyor General for the Minnesota District, was the first in a series of surveyors and scientists to work in the Itasca region. A leader at the Minnesota Historical Society, he vigorously contested Glazier's claim that Elk Lake was the source of the Mississippi. In his 1887 report, "The Sources of the Mississippi: Their Discoverers, Real and Pretended," he presented data that supported Itasca as the true source.

AN OFFICIAL GOVERNMENT SURVEY

Edwin S. Hall performed the official government survey of the area in 1875. Forging a crude road through the dense wilderness, he came from Little Mantrap Lake to a campsite on the north shore of Hernando DeSoto Lake opposite Brower Island, likely in the neighborhood of today's backcountry campsite there. His survey, focused around major lakes, outlined boundaries for land claims and led to the "pine rush" of timber cruisers who followed in his wake. After completing his survey, Hall stated that Elk Lake was the source of the Mississippi River.

THE FIRST SERMON PREACHED ON THE LAKE

In May 1881, Rev. J. A. Gilfillan, Episcopal missionary to White Earth, walked from his mission church in White Earth to the Nicollet Basin and Lake Itasca, guided by Sha-wun-uk-u-mig. He named Whipple Lake after Episcopal Bishop Henry Whipple, founder of churches and Indian missions throughout the state. Whipple had advocated for the 303 Dakota who were condemned to death after the Dakota Conflict of 1862, leading to President Lincoln's pardon of 265 of them. Brower reported that Rev. Gilfillan preached the first sermon on the shore of Lake Itasca near Elk Lake, based on the text, "Then had Thy peace been as a river."

DEBUNKING GLAZIER ONCE AGAIN

In a continuing effort to determine the true source of the Mississippi, and partly in reaction to Willard Glazier's claims that Elk Lake ("Lake Glazier") was the source, Hopewell Clarke and two assistants surveyed the flow in Nicollet Creek and the feeders of Elk Lake in 1886. He concluded that Whipple Lake fed Nicollet Creek through underground connections, but that Nicollet's Upper Lake was now a dry bed. Clarke mistakenly located the height of land to be just south of Whipple Lake, rather than south of Hernando DeSoto Lake, where it belongs, but otherwise did manage to shed some light on the topic with his lengthy publication in *Science* later that year, which showed that Nicollet Creek accounted for about three-quarters of the surface flow into Lake Itasca.

THE FIRST TOURISTS TO THE LAKE

Other early visitors, who could be considered the first "tourists" to Lake Itasca, included Charles Lanman and Allan Morrison, William's brother, in 1846; Rev. Frederick Ayer in 1849; A. H. Siegfried, who led the "Rob Roy" expedition and O. E. Garrison, who was lost for 13 days in the vicinity of Little Mantrap Lake. Brower states that a "Mr. Bungo" visited Itasca in 1865. This is most likely George Bonga, a highly regarded fur trader of mixed African and Ojibwe heritage, fluent in English, French and Ojibwe, who served as an interpreter for Lewis Cass in 1820 and accompanied him to Cass Lake. Bonga's name also appears on the Treaty of 1867 at White Earth. He called himself one of the first two white men in northern Minnesota, a reflection of the attitude in the fur-trading community at the time that anyone who was not Indian was "white" and therefore could claim the status of a fur trader.

HON. J. V. BROWER, COMMISSIONER.

Jacob V. Brower

The Fight for Itasca State Park

Jacob V. Brower, accompanied by John Leyendecker and William Avery, first visited Lake Itasca on October 19, 1888, for a "casual examination" of the area and to survey the flow of streams that entered the lake. Their exploration was triggered in part by Willard Glazier's wild claims from his 1881 expedition, when he "determined" that Elk Lake was the source of the Mississippi. Brower first arrived in Minnesota at age 16 when his family moved from Michigan to Long Prairie, Minnesota, in 1860. Initially a schoolteacher, he served in the First Minnesota Cavalry in 1862, was a seaman in the Navy, and went on to work as the Todd County Auditor, a legislator and an attorney. He also did archaeological research from Wisconsin to Missouri, in the Rocky Mountain region and explored the source of the Missouri River.

A MORE THOROUGH LOOK AT ITASCA

On February 12, 1889, Brower was commissioned by the Minnesota Historical Society to do a detailed survey of the water and land of the entire Lake Itasca watershed. His work, which set the stage for the establishment of the park, was poorly financed and he was forced to pay most of the costs out of his own pocket. He enlisted a number of assistants to map the hydrology and land in great detail; his crew included several Park Rapids residents and settlers already at Lake Itasca. They began their survey a month later and continued until October.

Hernando DeSoto Lake, Brower Island

HEADWATERS ARE HARD TO DEFINE

What constitutes a river's source? Is it the first drops of water from a spring, the trickle of a stream, or must it be a lake? Could Hernando DeSoto Lake or Whipple Lake, connected to the Headwaters via underground flowage, be considered the source? Can Nicollet Lake, Elk Lake or Mary Lake, all of which feed Lake Itasca, be singled out? Brower noted that various rivers of the world have all had varying criteria applied to determine their sources, and that there was no single, widely accepted definition. So he concluded, "in the absence of any fundamental term upon which to proceed, a reliable rule of no uncertainty, the rule dictated by nature, in ascertaining where the waters were gathered which form the remotest source of the Mississippi, was adopted . . ." In other words, you choose what best fits your concept of "source," and go with it.

DEBUNKING GLAZIER

Brower's detailed map and studies of the water flow and patterns around Lake Itasca and Elk Lake determined that Lake Itasca was the best choice as the true source, due to the flow from multiple streams, including Nicollet Creek, which provided the most water, as well as other inlets, including Chambers Creek from Elk Lake, and Mary Creek, Boutwell Creek and French Creek. Brower, eager to refute Glazier's claims that Elk Lake was the source, documented that the drought of 1889 reduced Chambers Creek to a depth of one inch with "imperceptible flow" by September. He reported that Peter Turnbull in 1883–1884 "walked up the bed of the creek without wetting the soles of his shoes." Yet there was always a current into the Mississippi River from Lake Itasca, greatly exceeding the flow from all the feeder streams combined, suggesting that underground sources provide the lake with much of its water. Modern hydrologic studies have proven that he was right and, in fact, show that over half of Lake Itasca's water is spring-fed.

ITASCA BECOMES AN OFFICIAL STATE PARK

During his detailed survey, Brower recognized what a natural treasure he was exploring and began his efforts to establish a state park to protect the timber, wildlife and other natural resources in the area. On March 2, 1891, General John Sanborn from Ramsey County introduced Brower's bill, S.F. 461, to establish the park. A similar request to the federal government was denied, as lands in the area had already been sold. As the timber industry was the major economic engine in the state, and many in the legislature and higher levels of state government were closely connected with it, Brower's efforts to deny loggers access to such a significant area was met with strident opposition. The bill passed the Senate only after vigorous lobbying, and even then only by a single vote. And it passed only after acceptance of an amendment to pay the park commissioner for just 60 days with no mention of future payment, a measure that opponents of the idea laughingly assumed would ultimately kill it. The bill was rushed through the House at the end of the session and, after the House sponsor threatened to recall it over a political slight, more delicate negotiation produced a quick signature by Governor Merriam. At that moment, "there was not a single acre of park land nor a cent of money in its fund." Anticipating the struggle ahead, Jacob V. Brower accepted the job of Commissioner of Itasca State Park, a "park on paper."

MONEY WOES

Initially Brower had to use his own funds to begin the work of setting up the park and even to acquire land. The Northern Pacific Railroad sold its land for 50¢ an acre, but lumber interests opposed the idea from the onset and insisted on top dollar. Timber operations had acquired some land in the park through direct purchase, and more by having their own employees "homestead" 160 acres each and then sell the land to the company. Attempts to secure an appropriation in 1893 ended in defeat, but Brower was defiant, declaring on the capitol portico that "Itasca Park shall live forever." He pressed on, and by the end of his term, December 1, 1894, he had spent $5,100 of his own funds on behalf of the state. When he later in disgust declined an offer by the legislature to cover half of the amount, "vituperative and disrespectful language was all the reward the commissioner received for his four years of arduous labors."

DEDICATION TO THE END

Brower completed a timber survey in 1895 and 1900, detailing the extent and nature of the old forests, and showing how much money would be needed to acquire the land and protect the big pines within the park. His field work was intense and physically exhausting, a measure of the depth of his dedication to the preservation of the park. Having laid the groundwork for Itasca State Park by exploring and documenting its geology, archaeology, forests and waters—his "long struggle and unselfish devotion"—Brower died in 1905. Itasca park commissioners after Brower were: A. A. Whitney (1895–1899), William P. Christensen (1899–1900), John P. Gibbs (1901–1903), Mary H. Gibbs (acting, 1903), and C. E. Bullard (1903–1906).

THE LIND SADDLE TRAIL

Inspired by Governor John Lind in 1899 and cleared by a crew under the supervision of Jacob Brower, the original Lind Saddle Trail began near the future site of Douglas Lodge and initially covered 13 miles. The trail followed the wagon road to Park Rapids south of Mary Creek and proceeded along the west side of Mary Lake (today's Ozawindib Trail) to Budd Lake, near the present-day location of Red Pine and Okerson Heights Trails. From there it went to Gilfillan Lake and, via today's Eagle Scout Trail, to Hernando DeSoto Lake, north to Whipple and Nicollet Lakes, and then to Elk Springs, Aiton Heights and back to Mary Lake, where it returned to the north shore of Lake Itasca. With the addition of spur trails to Morrison Lake and a short detour to the Ramsey Pine by Whipple Lake, the trail was completed in 1900 and marked with a wooden signpost each mile. The markers were later changed to concrete monuments with a wooden plaque attached, and some of them are still present along today's hiking trails.

Brower's description of the park at the time still applies today. He described the park's "beautifully wild and magnificent forest scenes, interspersed with creeks, lakes, heights, surface depressions, springs, thickets, fir and pine groves, deep ravines and glacial hills." Brower hoped that the park's "elegant views and scenes" would be so attractive that it would confirm the wisdom of completing and preserving the state park.

JOHN AND MARY GIBBS

John Gibbs, appointed the fourth commissioner in 1901, was unsuccessful in stopping construction of a logging dam at the Headwaters, even as land condemnation proceedings for the 160-acre tract were underway so that the state could acquire the land around the Mississippi River outlet. The timber industry needed access to Lake Itasca, which was a valuable reservoir for log storage; during the winter, it held logs harvested from Itasca State Park's land and the surrounding area. In spring, the logs were floated to Lake Irvine at Bemidji.

Mary H. Gibbs

MARY H. GIBBS.

FIGHTING FOR THE PARK, AND A NEW GIBBS TAKES OVER

Although he had made efforts to protect and develop the park, Gibbs fought an uphill, underfunded battle. The State Auditor's office even noted that his son, David Gibbs, illegally cut timber from park lands and sold them to Bonness & Co. When John Gibbs resigned due to terminal kidney disease in January of 1903, his 24-year-old daughter Mary, who had assisted him in his daily tasks, was appointed Park Commissioner. By then the logging dam built by the Mississippi-Schoolcraft Boom and Improvement Company had backed up the water on Itasca, Elk and Nicollet Lakes and was threatening to drown the trees on low ground along the shoreline of those lakes, especially in cedar and tamarack wetlands around Boutwell Creek and similar areas.

Logs on Lake Itasca

UNTRUSTWORTHY LOGGERS

Condemnation proceedings had been completed in December 1902, so the land was by then under state jurisdiction. Attorney General Douglas had attempted to negotiate leaving the dam at 18 inches above the normal water level, in a bargain to protect timber in other areas, but loggers built the dam higher anyway. After corresponding several times with Douglas for his direction, Mary Gibbs decided to take action. When she first confronted the dam operators, they promised to act in two days. But when she returned three days later, on April 14, 1903, the water was up nearly two feet above normal and the frost was out of the ground, leaving wide areas of flooded trees vulnerable to damage. The loggers obligingly lifted the gate, but closed it again as soon as she had left.

RETURNING WITH REINFORCEMENTS—AND A WARRANT

Mary Gibbs returned the next day with Constable Heinzelman and a warrant for the arrest of the three men in charge. They were defiant, and according to Mary, "M. A. ['Wolf'] Woods drew a revolver on the constable." In a letter to author John Dobie in 1956, Gibbs recalled that Woods said, "I'll shoot anyone who puts a hand on those levers." She replied, "I will put my hand on there and you will not shoot it off either." And she did, although she could not raise the gates, "as it took about six men to do that." She contacted the Clearwater County Sheriff, who arrested two of the men. Again the gate was opened, and again it was closed as soon as the sheriff left. The boom company then sued for an injunction against her in district court, claiming that Mary Gibbs had "with a strong hand and a multitude of people, maliciously and wrongfully threatened and intimidated said employees [sic] . . . in a loud boisterous and threatening manner, demanded that said gates be raised." Judge M. A. Spooner, apparently ignoring the fact that the company was trespassing on park property, agreed, and signed the injunction preventing Mary Gibbs from interfering with the dam on April 20, 1903.

Sluicing Logs, 1906

THE AFTERMATH OF THE INJUNCTION

Bob Mitchell, who was in charge of the dam crew, later confirmed that, "Permission to build the dam had been applied for but had not been granted." He said that the lake was floating 1½–2 million feet of logs, although others reported up to 9 million feet that year. After the injunction was filed against Gibbs, Mitchell related, "I had instructions from the company to start sluicing, which I did. By the time they got the argument settled I had all the logs through the dam" and on their way to Lake Irvine near Bemidji. Once the logs were through, the company, having achieved its goals, lowered the dam, which had reached three feet above normal water level, back down to the agreed-upon 18-inch limit and withdrew the injunction against Mary Gibbs. She resigned her post on April 28, and C. E. Bullard took over as park superintendent. Mary Gibbs never returned to Itasca and kept hidden all the pictures that she had taken of the early days of the park. After moving to Minneapolis and later to Vancouver, British Columbia, Canada, Mary Gibbs Logan lived to the age of 104. After her death, her grandchildren discovered the photos hidden in a trunk and donated them to Itasca State Park, where they are now extensively used in interpretive displays.

ITASCA STATE PARK— LOGGING AND PRESERVATION

Connor and Wilson Logging Camp

During the entire 1901 session, Rep. J. H. O'Neil of Park Rapids fought for a $5,000-per-year appropriation for the park in order to continue the land acquisition and development process. Rep. P. C. Deming reported an ongoing battle with Mr. J. F. Jacobson, the chairman of the appropriations committee, who was finally overcome by the efforts of Deming, O'Neil and Dr. L. W. Babcock of Wadena. Despite this, during most of the years following Mary Gibbs' brief tenure as Park Commissioner, those in control of the park were sympathetic to lumber interests and did little to stop them. Large companies owned by Weyerhauser (Pine Tree Lumber) and T. B. Walker (Red River Lumber) remained committed to logging as much as possible of the big pines before they moved on to choicer properties out west. Due to the logging companies' asking price for the land (twice the estimated value) and the very limited state funds that had been appropriated, attempts at negotiations through 1903 had failed. In a letter to Attorney General Douglas in June 1903, Deming made a plea to condemn some of the land, especially along the east shore of Lake Itasca "ere the lumbermen, swooping down, as the Assyrians, 'like the wolf on the fold' get the start of us." Brower reported that by 1904 Itasca State Park was "given over to the lumbermen," with 10 million board feet of trees clogging the lake and precluding recreational use. He was appalled that Douglas, who had focused on acquiring land around the lakes that he liked the best, had done little to acquire more park lands and protect the ancient pine stands. By the time of Brower's death in 1905, the state owned less than 5,000 acres of the 20,000 within the original park boundary, and it would be fifteen years more before the remaining timberlands were acquired.

Scaling Defective Timber, Lake Itasca

ATTEMPTING TO PROTECT WHAT WAS LEFT

In 1907 the park was designated a state forest under the direction of the Forestry Board, and the Forestry School officially began classes in 1909. For the next twelve years the board did the best it could to acquire land and protect as much existing timber as possible. It purchased land from T. B. Walker, Pine Tree Lumber Company, Brainerd Lumber and Shevlin-Carpenter. Much of the land that had already been logged was donated to the park. The last major log drive in 1919 by Conner & Wilson removed timber from both sides of Elk Lake and the Middlewest Cabin area in the southwest corner of Wilderness Drive. A 2-mile strip of land along the west side of the park, which had already been completely logged by Pine Tree Lumber and Red River Lumber, was added in 1919, bringing Itasca State Park close to its current boundaries. Today the logged-over areas have filled in with mature aspen, maple and younger red and white pines. Virgin forest still stands in scattered patches to large tracts, thanks to the efforts of Jacob V. Brower, Mary Gibbs and others like them who had the vision and courage to preserve these remnants of natural grandeur.

Peter and Mary Turnbull Family

Early Settlers

The first group of white settlers to move into what is now Itasca State Park was led by Peter and Mary Turnbull, who homesteaded on the east side of Lake Itasca near Peace Pipe Vista in 1883. Peter, a surveyor and civil engineer, took the Hall Road of 1875 from west of Park Rapids north to Little Mantrap Lake. At the end of that road he and his crew blazed a new road near Lake Frazier, running along the east side of Gilfillan Lake, through Iron Corner, and north along the west side of the Mary Valley, the route of today's Ozawindib and Mary Lake Trails. One year later, their son Charley was born, and in 1885 they moved back to Park Rapids.

THE PATTERSON FARM

Just north of the current museum, David S. Patterson homesteaded along Lake Itasca in 1889, purchasing another 152 acres in 1891 that included the Headwaters. An interpretive plaque marks the site of his old farm.

Feeding Elk

THE MCMULLEN RANCH AND A FATAL CASE OF MISTAKEN IDENTITY

William McMullen settled on the north end of the lake in 1889, also near the museum. His log cabin, which developed into the McMullen Ranch, served hundreds of tourists, timber cruisers, scientists and others. He built a new road in 1894 and in 1898 donated land for a community cemetery, preserved today as the Itasca Pioneer Cemetery. Nine-year-old Luise Rohrich, daughter of a homesteader to the northwest, was the first to be buried there in 1898. McMullen himself was the second, as announced in the *Park Rapids Enterprise* headline, "Killed for a Deer!" He and his neighbor Nelson Rust went hunting for white-tailed deer, which were scarce in those days, and the two became separated after entering the dense woods. McMullen's wife had wrapped him in a white scarf for warmth, but when he plunged into the brush in pursuit of a bear they had flushed, Rust saw a flash of white in the brush, mistook McMullen for a deer, and shot, killing him nearly instantly. Although the newspaper reported that Rust was "nearly beside himself with grief," McMullen's friends didn't believe his story, and Rust was accused of murder. The grand jury excused him on the basis of insufficient evidence—the defense showed that a picture of the site purporting to show an open area appeared to be doctored—but McMullen's friends and the Rust family remained at odds for decades, leading to a famous feud.

A FEUD IS SETTLED

Historian John Dobie recounted stories of the sometimes-violent feud between the Rusts and the McMullens. When the clash was finally settled in the mid-1930s with a gift of Texas grapefruit from Martin Heinzelman, a relative of Rust, to Theodore Wegmann, one of McMullen's friends, Wegmann reacted first with tears of gratitude, then said, "I bet they are poisoned." Forester Frank Pugh had to try a few to prove otherwise.

THE WEGMANN STORE

Wegmann Store Reconstruction

Although the original Weg-mann Store is now a pile of logs returning to the earth, the recon-structed building gives one a hint of what it was like when Theodore and Johanna built their log cabin in 1893 and later the general store, which became the Lake Itasca Post Office in 1895. They provided for tourists, neighbors and residents of the CCC camps in the 1930s. The store also offered meals and lodging, and business gradually increased over the years until summers became very busy for them. Wegmann also served as a diligent game warden in the area for 25 years. The *Park Rapids Enterprise* reported in 1921 that he followed a wolf into the brush one day, only to encounter two exhausted white-tailed bucks, which had locked antlers during a battle and were unable to separate. He struggled to help them, and finally, with assistance, was able to saw one of the antler prongs off and free the two.

Early settlers occasionally had a rough time with large predators, as this account from the *Akeley Tribune* suggests: Mrs. Henselman was passing through timber near Lake Itasca when she "was suddenly confronted by a huge lynx, preparing to spring upon her." She brought her rifle to her shoulder and shot it once, then several more times as it came toward her. It was a "monster, measuring six feet in length." "Mrs. Hinselman [sic] is a crack shot, and is said to have become so thru innumerable shooting contests with her husband, as to which one should arise on the next morning to build the kitchen fire. The husband usually builds the fire."

BERT'S CABINS

Wegmann's nephew, Bert Pfeifer, moved from North Dakota in 1939 and bought the 40 acres that is still the site of Bert's Cabins, now run by Bert's daughter Pat Evenwoll and her husband, Dave. Johanna Wegmann's brother, August Schneider, came to Itasca in 1894 and worked at the Wegmann Store and also for the Connors and Wilson Logging Company on Lake Ozawindib. In 1912 he built a resort, Parkview Lodge, which was popular into the 1930s but no longer exists.

Matson's Cabin

MORE HOME-STEADERS AND A WOLF ATTACK

Homesteader Ernest Sauer and his family operated a store and cabins near the north entrance to the park. John Dobie reported Sauer's tale of a wolf attack one evening, as he returned with a load of groceries from Wegmann's store. Sauer climbed a tree and threw lighted matches at the wolves, which finally left. After dashing home without his groceries, he called for help from Wegmann and three others to retrieve them. Sauer assumed Wegmann's position as postmaster in 1919, and the Lake Itasca Post Office, which was located at today's intersection of MN-200 and Clearwater County 2, remained open until 1992. Mail is now delivered to area residents in a collection of outdoor post boxes. Theodore Wegmann died in 1941 and was buried in Pioneer Cemetery in Itasca State Park. The park purchased his 160-acre farm in 1945, incorporating it into the park.

Frank Mitchell's Jefferson
Highway Marker

The Jefferson Highway

In the early 1900s, as automobiles began to motor through the primitive streets and roads that had been designed for the horse and buggy, groups of hardy motorists braved the dirt-and-gravel roads and took long excursions across the country. The novelty of speedy travel without the need for horses spurred a new era of discovery, and automobile associations sponsored routes nation-wide. It was in that spirit that the Jefferson Highway Association established a route from New Orleans, Louisiana, to Winnipeg, Manitoba, in 1915. Of the various competing routes in Minnesota, the middle one through Park Rapids, Itasca State Park and Bemidji finally won out in 1916 as part of the official "Pine to Palm" highway that crossed the central part of the nation. (Detroit Lakes lost out, but kept the label for its golf club and tournament.)

THE JEFFERSON HIGHWAY

The Jefferson Highway followed some of the old wagon roads to Itasca, although the original route, which began 4 miles west of Park Rapids and meandered north, was not ideal for modern travel. J. V. Brower reported in 1904 that the road was 23 miles long, and the trip could be made in 3–5 hours in good weather, "depending upon the character of the conveyance and disposition of the driver." By 1916 the road, which was curvy, hilly and rough, had been moved and straightened at least three times to an alignment close to today's US-71. Local historian Frank Mitchell reports that the Jefferson Highway roughly followed the route of today's South Entrance Road through the park to Douglas Lodge. From there the road traveled north to Becida and Bemidji, and on through St. Vincent to Winnipeg. Later maps show the route running more directly to Becida from Itasca's East Entrance, although a 1926 park map has it following Main Park Drive to the Headwaters and leaving Itasca State Park to the north.

A SOCIAL OCCASION FOR ALL

The first "Sociability Run" from St. Joseph, Missouri, to Winnipeg rumbled through Park Rapids in late July 1916, shortly after the adoption of the central Minnesota route. Travelers made their way through crowds of enthusiastic local residents in Menahga and Park Rapids. An arch draped in pine boughs and flags over 2nd St. and Main Ave. declared Park Rapids "Gateway to Itasca State Park." The travelers were joined on their trip through Park Rapids by 150 local automobiles from the surrounding area, each sporting a pennant that read, "Park Rapids, we like it, you'll like it." The tourists continued on to Itasca, where they had dinner at Douglas Lodge.

THE END OF THE JEFFERSON HIGHWAY

The Jefferson Highway route continued into the late 1920s, when other state and national highway designations began to take over. A plaque describing the history of the Jefferson Highway stands at the site of Arago, a ghost village on the corner of Hubbard County 41 and US-71 near Two Inlets. The highway encouraged road improvements, which spurred tourism and brought increasing numbers of visitors to Itasca State Park.

Lake Itasca CCC Camp, "52 Below"

Civilian Conservation Corps in Itasca

Walking up the broad flagstone path to the Forest Inn, you approach walls of expertly crafted split rock. The rectangular cut design covers the foundation to your left and the entire wall on the wing to your right. Massive logs anchor the roof. Note the corner logs of the building with their characteristic three-sided cut. Step inside the doors to the warm lobby and look around at the carefully designed patterns in stone, woodwork and logs, which have changed little since they were placed. You are surrounded by the legacy of the Veterans Conservation Corps (VCC) and the Civilian Conservation Corps (CCC) and craftsmanship at its finest.

THE CIVILIAN CONSERVATION CORPS IS CREATED

During his first month in office in 1933, President Franklin Delano Roosevelt pushed through and signed the Emergency Conservation Work Act authorizing the CCC. Minnesota and the rest of the country slogged through the Great Depression. Unemployment rose to 29 percent, and families whose savings had been wiped out by bank failures and lack of income were struggling just to meet the basic needs of food and shelter. This program enrolled young men, who earned meals, clothing, shelter, medical care and $30 a month, $25 of which went home to their families. In exchange, they built roads, installed phone lines, planted trees and crops, cleared fire breaks, and, in Minnesota, constructed a lasting treasure of beautiful state park buildings.

THE BENEFITS OF THE CCC

When Murl McGrane entered a camp near his home in Sidney, Nebraska, "we didn't have nothin'," he says. Two years of drought and dust storms had decimated harvests and made life miserable and meager. "You could get surrounded by a huge swirling cloud of dust that would last for hours. When that happened, you'd better not move." But with the camps, that all changed. "I sent money home and put food on the table. We were lucky to have the CCC in Nebraska. We had something to do, and Mom and Dad had something to spend." Murl, who later moved to Minnesota, speared the large northern pike that now hangs on the wall of the Jacob V. Brower Visitor Center.

CAMP BUILDINGS

Sturdily constructed of wood frame buildings, the typical camp had barracks, a kitchen and dining hall, a schoolroom to help the boys keep up or catch up on their studies and an infirmary. The buildings were mostly uninsulated, which made for some hardship during the cold northern winters. "I was a fireman for one winter," recalls Leroy Czeczok, who planted trees and worked at camps in Ely, Nevis, and at Lovelis Lake, just southwest of Itasca. "I would warm up the kitchen at 4 a.m. and get the cooks up. Sometimes you had to feed the barrel stoves every hour." He admits that he got so homesick at the Ely camp that he and his buddies went "over the hill" one night. They took off after bedtime and headed for home, then thought better of it after they had walked many miles down the road. "We caught a ride back with the milk truck and went back to bed. We were all so happy to be back, and nobody even knew we were gone."

SOME MISCHIEVOUS ENTERTAINMENT

The Bagley Farmers Independent reported in 1935 that the end of the slot machine era took away a few CCC boys' devious entertainment. Discovering that a flattened metal "U.S. Army" uniform button was the same size and thickness as a dime, some of the boys from nearby camps would feed buttons into a dime slot machine, surrounding the machine so the operators couldn't see what they were doing. Playing till they won a jackpot, they would quickly weed out the buttons and walk home with full pockets. "Their little scheme kept slot machine operators pretty busy for a while."

RESTORING THE RIVER

Itasca had four CCC camps and two work camps within or near its borders. Camp Itasca (SP-1), first set up north of the Headwaters, moved to what is now Pine Ridge Campground and was reorganized as SP-19 in 1937. The workers' biggest assignment was the restoration of the outlet of Lake Itasca, which occurred from 1933 to 1941. Undoing the years of dredging, damming and straightening that the river had been subjected to by lumbermen, they followed a 1901 map to restore the river as closely as possible to its original alignment. For this they brought in 40,000 cubic yards of fill, rerouted the first half-mile of the channel, filled in swampy areas and planted 16 acres of trees in natural-looking groupings along the riverbanks. Their signature achievement was the concrete and rock dam at the outlet, 44 feet long and with over two feet of rock on top of the concrete. The project used weathered rock, designed to completely cover the concrete and look as natural as possible. It is now enjoyed by thousands of people every year, young and old, who can say, "I walked across the Mississippi River!"

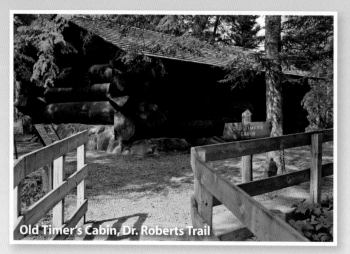

Old Timer's Cabin, Dr. Roberts Trail

THE OLD TIMER'S CABIN AND A TRANSITION TO THE VCC

The Old Timer's Cabin on the Dr. Roberts Trail was built in 1934 using trees that had fallen; the trees were so huge that the structure is only four logs high. The stone foundation is a good example of on-the-job training, as the work gets better the higher up you go! The camp changed to a Veterans Conservation Corps (VCC) facility in 1938, after which the Forest Inn was built, replacing the old Forest Inn and trading post of 1919. Thirty masons, all World War I veterans who had worked at Sibley State Park, took charge of stonework there. Most of the CCC/VCC buildings, including the log and stonework, were constructed by men from the local camps under the supervision of expert craftsmen. Ole Evenson managed the log construction, using pine and balsam fir from the park, and John Wiberg, the blacksmith foreman, created the ironwork for light fixtures and doors. This group also built the old East Contact Station (now East Cabin), several other cabins and structures, and a number of trails. This was one of the last CCC/VCC camps in the country, closing in the summer of 1942.

Ellersick Logging

FORESTRY WORK AND ONE LAST LOG DRIVE

The boys in Lovelis Lake Camp (S-57), located southwest of the park, concentrated on forestry projects, such as forest roads, firebreaks and tree planting. Their crews also worked on the Mary Lake Deer Exclosure and the construction of MN-113 and the Aiton Heights Fire Tower. Operating from 1933 to 1941, lumberjack George "Haywire" Wilson supervised the camp during the 1930s. In 1919, along with his partner Connor, Wilson had led the last log drive within Itasca's boundaries, cutting 9 million board feet of huge native pines near Elk Lake. Noted for his ability to fix anything and get tons of work done, Wilson was also famous for doing things his own way, ignoring all memos, letters and directives issued by his superiors and also ignoring the letters that chided him for ignoring orders.

ANNEX CAMP CONSTRUCTION

Annex Camp (SP-70) worked on road and forestry projects from its location near the east entrance. Two WPA work camps, located in what are now the Elk Lake and Lake Ozawindib group camps, improved Wilderness Drive using only shovels, pickaxes and pails. As you explore Itasca, you are likely to stumble upon CCC structures everywhere; they include the Douglas Lodge stone stairway (restored in 2014 after damage from the 2012 windstorm), drinking fountains, bathrooms, signs, cabins, sheds and even an old incinerator. Near the site of Annex Camp #70, just off East Entrance Road, there is even a section corner in split rock, with stone arrows that project from each face, indicating cardinal compass directions, with a tiny shelf to identify the north side. There were plans to build more section corners like this one, but the project, which began in 1941, was interrupted by World War II and the phasing out of the CCC.

Camp Rabideau

THE REMAINS OF THE CCC CAMPS

Only traces of the original CCC camps remain near Itasca. SP-19 is now Pine Ridge Campground, and a marker on MN-113 commemorates the old Lovelis Lake camp, which was originally located 1 mile north on Anchor Matson Road. If you would like to see what CCC camps were like, visit Camp Rabideau, 6 miles south of Blackduck on Beltrami County 39. Located in the Chippewa National Forest, the remaining buildings are being restored to their original appearance. Contact the U.S. Forest Service office in Blackduck or Cass Lake for current visitor information.

The Itasca Pageants, 1932–1938

In 1931 a group led by Park Superintendent Earl Lang gathered to plan an event to commemorate the 100th anniversary of Schoolcraft's arrival at Lake Itasca in 1832. Determined to prepare a celebration that would relieve some of the gloom of the Great Depression and draw new attention to Itasca State Park, they developed a series of pageants to be staged at the park to dramatize life prior to European settlement, including a traditional Ojibwe village, the life of trappers, soldiers and voyageurs, and Schoolcraft's journey from Sault Ste. Marie to Lake Itasca. Financed with a $100 contribution by each of the eleven communities around Itasca State Park, the events were quite an undertaking for park staff, who cleared the pageant grounds and constructed stockades, an Ojibwe village, roads, parking space and seating.

"Father of Waters"

A CAST OF CHARACTERS

The 1932 cast included 50 park and forestry staff members, plus University of Minnesota students and Boy Scouts. One hundred Ojibwe Indians participated and 35 Ojibwe from the White Earth Indian Reservation camped in birchbark wigwams July through early September. The rest were bused in from nearby reservations or homes on pageant days. In exchange for their participation, the Ojibwe were provided with their camp lodgings and board, collections from powwows and dances, money from the sale of handcrafts and tips from photographers. Described as "great actors and performers," they were, by some accounts, pleased to be a part of the pageants and many returned year after year.

THE FIRST PAGEANT

Over 2,500 people attended the first performance near the Mississippi Headwaters on July 13, 1932, 100 years from the day of Schoolcraft's arrival at Lake Itasca. The audience looked upon a village of Ojibwe, who were dressed in traditional attire and going about tasks of everyday life, as "Hotan Tonka" narrated the story of Indian life before settlement, and the subsequent incursions of European explorers, traders and trappers. Though pageants of that day were told mostly in pantomime, Itasca used sound amplification to broadcast the narration to the audience. One viewer, Donald Van Koughnet, described the scene: "Off to the right was visible an imposing wall of a stockaded trading post, through the gate of which passed the traders and the soldiers of the garrison in their daily routine. Directly in the background was the infant Mississippi meandering on its way to the distant sea, while stretching away to the left was the north arm of Lake Itasca. From time to time graceful Indian canoes and a stately Mackinaw boat were seen skirting the shore of the lake or gliding along the slender stream that was to become a mighty river . . ." The cast acted out the journey of Schoolcraft and his party from Sault Ste. Marie, as they traveled with their guide Ozawindib from Lake Superior to his Star Island village on Cass Lake, and finally to the Headwaters of the Mississippi at Lake Itasca.

A SERIES OF SUCCESSES

The pageants were a rousing success, attracting over 46,000 spectators to the six performances. Over 18,000 attended the July 31 presentation, overwhelming parking and picnic accommodations. Subsequent years highlighted other themes. The 1933 season opened with a cast supplemented by 200 Civilian Conservation Corps boys of Camp SP-1 decked out in period soldier uniforms of the First Minnesota Regiment of the Civil War. Titled the "Minnesota Diamond Jubilee Pageant," it celebrated 75 years of Minnesota's statehood. The cast of 500, including 200 Ojibwe, reenacted early Minnesota explorations of Du Luth, Radisson, and Father Hennepin, the establishment of Fort Snelling, the Dakota Conflict of 1862, and Indian enlistment in the Civil War. Over 40,000 visitors, half of them repeat attendees from 1932, filled Itasca State Park for the 1933 performances. A parking charge of 15¢ or 25¢ secured a spot in prime parking areas, but in true Minnesota fashion, workers were to "permit any car to enter without charge if the driver pleaded it was difficult to pay," and "not to argue if anyone disliked the idea of paying 25¢." The entire cast was trucked down to Whitewater State Park in southeastern Minnesota for a special performance on August 20, 1933, where attendance was estimated at 25,000–40,000.

FROM 1934 TO 1938

The pageants continued, as 59,000 viewed the 1934 series about Henry Sibley, Minnesota's first governor. Lloyd Schrum was 8 years old when his neighbor brought him to the 1935 pageant highlighting the fur trade, to help relieve some of the stress from his father's recent stroke. "I remember a mock war, a dance and a powwow. Some of the Indians had beautiful headdresses, and the chief wore one that stretched all the way down his back." On July 12, 1936, during a pageant featuring a tribute to the first missionaries, a troop of Boy Scouts from Oslo, Norway, along with scouts from surrounding communities, were welcomed as they marched out onto the pageant grounds. The 1937 performances, with visitors from over 30 states, featured the creation of Lake Itasca as told in Indian folklore. With a recession in 1938 and the threat of war in Europe looming on the horizon, a single program in late summer about the exploration of the Northwest Territory, "Freedom to March," brought the years of pageantry to an end.

Swimming Beach Building

Park Buildings and Development

DOUGLAS LODGE

Douglas Lodge is the first memorable Rustic Style building in any Minnesota state park and was constructed by T. C. Myers and his son, Samuel, of Park Rapids, in 1904. It was dedicated in June 1905. The Myers family also built several homes, churches, and the Carnegie Library in Park Rapids. The original lodge, 40x80 feet in size, contained sixteen rooms and one large parlor with several windows and a stone fireplace. Built on a stone foundation, the lumber came from downed timber in the park, at a cost of $8. The lodge was named for Honorable Wallace B. Douglas, the state Attorney General, who encouraged its construction when he first visited the park with Governor Lind in 1899. T. C. Myers was paid $5,025 for his share of the work, and the total cost of the finished lodge was $10,000. The Myers originally designed the lodge as a residence for the park commissioner, and it included steam heat, running water and room to house and entertain guests.

Douglas Lodge sketch

A DELAYED DEDICATION

When state officials dedicated Douglas Lodge in 1905, local residents marked each mile of the road from Park Rapids with a boulder with mileage painted black on a white background. The road was primitive, delaying the dedication trip, as "incessant rains of the past month had left the roads in such condition that it was not deemed advisable." So Attorney General Douglas and Governor Johnson returned to Park Rapids, where they were met by the community band and escorted to the courthouse for the ceremony.

A GRAND LODGE

With its view overlooking the South Arm of Lake Itasca on the ridge—not far from where Schoolcraft and Nicollet first arrived at the lake—Douglas Lodge was a big hit from the start with visitors. Easier to access than the original "State House" on the north end of the lake, Douglas Lodge was described by guest

Bertha Severtson as "the loveliest spot in Minnesota, where one finds health and perfect contentment." The Clubhouse and nearby Cabin 11 were added in 1911 and restored in the 1980s. The Clubhouse logs were set with a hollowed-out groove over the length of the underside of each log, which precluded the need for chinking. Envisioned as a grand lodge, like those found in national parks, the entire complex sported recreational amenities as evidenced by its golf course, which was used into the 1940s. Blueprints outlined a short, five-hole layout that might be considered a "pitch and putt" by today's standards.

CHANGES OVER THE YEARS

Douglas Lodge has undergone many changes and updates over the years, but the character in this original, classic Rustic Style park structure remains. Railings have been replaced, trees thinned and replanted in 1940, and roads and drives have been moved and redone over the years. Some cabins were added from 1910 to 1925, and the Civilian Conservation Corps built others. Original Rustic Style cabins have two angled cuts on log ends, CCC cabins have three, and cabins from the 1950s have board and batten siding. The veranda, enclosed by sliding windows in 1952, is now the restaurant, where today's diners still have a wonderful view of Lake Itasca. The kitchen has been updated to modern standards and additional dining space added, while still preserving the original look of the building.

Mississippi Headwaters AYH-Hostel

FROM HEAD-QUARTERS TO A HOSTEL

Mississippi Headwaters Hostel now occupies the Old Park Headquarters of 1923, which originally housed the park superintendent and provided kitchen and dining facilities for staff. The CCC completed a new headquarters in 1941, which was used as Itasca State Park Headquarters until the Jacob V. Brower Visitor Center was opened.

Itasca State Park was listed on the National Register in 1973 and its listing was updated in 1992, with 72 buildings listed as Historic Places, most of which date back to the Douglas Lodge development or the Civilian Conservation Corps era from 1933 to 1941. One hidden treasure not on this list is an old split rock section corner, located on a side trail just north of the East Entrance Road. In 1941 the CCC had planned more corners like this, but the outbreak of World War II ended the project, leaving this small structure as the only example in Itasca.

White Pine Seedling

Mizpah Survey Crew

HERE 1475 FT
ABOVE
THE OCEAN
THE MIGHTY
MISSISSIPPI
BEGINS
TO FLOW
ON ITS
WINDING WAY
2552 MILES
TO THE
GULF OF
MEXICO

Headwaters Signpost

Modern History

This section highlights some of the changes that have taken place in Itasca State Park in recent years.

Park development paused in the 1940s as the state and nation recovered from World War II. Then in the 1950s the park began expanding services and facilities to meet the changing needs of an ever more mobile population. The hiking and driving trails were adapted for activities, such as bicycling, skiing and snowmobiling, and campgrounds were modernized to accommodate trailers and motor homes. New visitor centers have kept Itasca State Park in the forefront of state park development and programming.

Jacob V. Brower Visitor Center

Jacob V. Brower Visitor Center

Itasca Up to the Present Day

Following the CCC-inspired explosion of building and development in the 1930s, Itasca changed little for many years. During World War II the Lake Ozawindib Camp (formerly Squaw Lake Camp) was used by the Air Force as a rest camp, although rumors of a German POW camp there were never confirmed. After the war ended, fire destroyed the kitchen and mess hall as the camp was being shut down for the winter. In 1949 the Air Force sent Itasca State Park a check for $6,819 to reconstruct the kitchen and dining hall, and the facility grew into what is now the Lake Ozawindib Group Center.

EXPANSION BEGINS AGAIN

By the late 1950s the park once again began expanding services for the growing numbers of summer visitors. Carl Johnson built Brower Inn in 1958, a mid-century modern design with a low-pitched roof and wide expanses of glass. Located on a hillside near the swimming beach, it served as a snack bar, souvenir shop and restaurant for decades. Visitors to the lower level walked out through beautiful split-rock granite stonework to a level lawn, leading down CCC-era stone steps to a pier on Lake Itasca. The snack bar was a bustling destination for summer tourists. Lorraine Vojak, who has worked at Itasca since 1967, said, "When the beach crowd hit the lower level, we would be busy making malts and shakes." The gift shop upstairs later became a full restaurant and was also used for art exhibits and other events. However, the new gift shop and food service building at the Headwaters began to take over more of the functions of Brower Inn, and it gradually fell into disuse. Lorraine said, "It was built on stilts" (pilings), on soft ground that was underlain with springs, so it had to be heated year-round to keep the roof and glass from shifting. The building became too expensive to maintain and was finally removed in the early 2000s.

CHIEF LITTLECREEK

The first Headwaters gift shop was a small building located near the Headwaters. Ben Littlecreek, an Ojibwe from Red Lake, was caretaker at the Mississippi Headwaters Museum in the picnic area in the 1950s and early 1960s. After sweeping up each morning, he would don his full ceremonial regalia and walk or drive to the Headwaters. "Chief Littlecreek" appeared nearly daily in the summer for years, selling souvenirs, postcards and photo-ops to tourists. Ben Thoma, park naturalist at the time, recounts that Ben would put headdresses on children and pose for pictures with them. He would hold his hand out and state, "FIFTY CENTS, not compulsory," the last two words almost inaudible.

Mary Gibbs Mississippi Headwaters Center

Ben Littlecreek died in 1964, and in the late 1960s the park moved the parking area and approach away from the immediate area of the outlet and built a new gift shop and cafeteria. The Mary

Gibbs Mississippi Headwaters Center replaced that facility in 2005. An inviting canopy shelters a huge 3-D map of the Mississippi River and interpretive displays that people can enjoy even when the building is closed. With a large cafeteria and gift shop, it hosts naturalist events, music and good-sized groups.

THE TINY TOWN OF LAKE ITASCA

Changes continued after World War II for the small community of Lake Itasca, just north of the park boundary. Business at the historic resorts improved at first, but the resorts later began to disappear and were absorbed into the state park. Heinzelman's Headwaters Inn, with accommodations for 45, had several cabins on the east side of the Mississippi River and a hotel on the west side, until it was sold to the park in the 1950s and demolished. The site now holds the tiny self-serve North Entrance station. Across the highway to the north, Ernest and Anne Sauer developed a general store, post office and Pine Grove Cabins, which were built in palisade style with vertical log sides. The adjacent baseball diamond was a popular gathering place on summer evenings, hosting teams from White Earth and other nearby communities. The Lake Itasca Store closed in 2003, and Itasca RV Park and Campground now operates there.

DOING THINGS THE HARD WAY

Dorothy Katzenmeyer, who moved to Lake Itasca with her late husband Alvin in the 1940s, raised a large family in the house that he constructed. Building on the site of the first CCC camp near Itasca, he first cobbled it together out of Wegmann's tool shed and granary and later expanded and updated it. Dorothy became postmaster in 1972, serving Lake Itasca for 20 years. When she retired in 1992, the post office closed. Dick Sauer, who had originally helped construct the post office building, dismantled it and rebuilt it again on the grounds of the Lake Itasca Pioneer Farmers Village nearby, on land that had been purchased from the Katzenmeyers. On the day that I visited with her she was still happily living in her modernized home and had enjoyed the visit of a mother bear and three cubs the previous evening, feasting on acorns beneath the two magnificent oaks in her yard.

THE WEGMANN STORE

The Wegmann Store was extremely busy during the Pageants of the 1930s and would sell up to 40 gallons of ice cream a day. Theodore Wegmann was noted for not wanting people in bathing suits wandering into his store. When the Wegmann Store closed after Theodore Wegmann's death in 1941, the building was moved to Parkview Resort, which operated until it burned down in the 1960s. The Stevens Corner resort, which operated into the 1950s, was notable for one of its residents, a Lebanese salesman named Abdulla, who sold clothing from his car for many years.

ST. CATHERINE'S CATHOLIC CHURCH

Father Joseph Fraling, using materials salvaged from old buildings, began building St. Catherine's Catholic Church in 1941. His hand-stenciled designs adorn the small sanctuary, which still fills with worshipers every Sunday at 9 a.m. during the summer months and at a special early-morning mass during the first weekend of deer season.

PINE RIDGE CAMPGROUND

With continued pressure for more overnight lodging, park staff transformed the former CCC camp into Pine Ridge Campground, which opened as a rustic overflow campground in 1961 and developed into a fully functioning facility by 1969. Like all CCC camps, it was initially wide open and cleared of vegetation, although the trees have gradually filled in and matured. Douglas Lodge also expanded services, with Cabins 1, 14 and 15 opening in the 1950s. The architect's drawing shows a mid-century modern design, but the cabins were built with a more traditional look while retaining the low-pitched roof typical of 1950s architecture. Until the Douglas Lodge Itasca (Four Season) Suites came on the scene more recently, all of the Douglas Lodge options were built without any kitchen or housekeeping facilities, with the idea that visitors would get their meals at Douglas Lodge or elsewhere. Although there was talk of developing a new campground northwest of Douglas Lodge about twenty years ago, those plans never progressed, and it is likely that the overnight capacity of the park won't increase in the future. Referring to the continued pressure to expand capacity, Reuben Law, landscape architect during the CCC era, stated, "It doesn't matter how many buildings and campgrounds you build, you will not be able to preserve the Park until you can control use." Myrtie Hunt, who worked at Douglas Lodge for several summers as a student, said, "I'm always afraid of too much development because it tramples on the ecology. Do not trample on the ecology . . . That's first, not the money."

THE ITASCA ZOO

At one time the "Itasca Zoo" held elk, bison and even a pair of bears in pens near the picnic grounds. The buffalo pens were popular with tourists during the 1950s and 1960s. Initially located along the lakeshore so the buffalo could walk into the lake, they were later moved across the road. Keith Butler, in an interview with Amy Rieger, recalled that, "We used to go down and feed them and get them to charge the fence. They would actually charge us and run into the fence and we used to think that was a great joy." The elk were initially contained in a pasture between the east and west arms of Lake Itasca and were later in a pen, but were difficult to manage. "The elk would get out, then the local farmers would get together . . . and drive them, chase them, corral them, get them back into the fence . . . Finally the farmers were getting very exasperated with it." The elk were moved out of the park in the 1930s. The bears were penned in, with a den that the CCC boys had dug into the hillside. Elon Cary had to go into the pen to throw in hay one fall, and "the she-bear came out. Her eyes were just as red as fire and she was mad . . . When she came down, her claws grabbed the back of my jacket and tore my jacket. The buttons flew off and I let her have the jacket and I ran on."

Naturalist Tour, Forest Inn

A NATURALIST HELPS DEFINE ITASCA

The Park Naturalist program has always been the heart of Itasca's interpretive efforts, giving visitors an in-depth look at the cultural and natural history of the region. Ben Thoma, who was the first biology professor at Willmar Community College, learned about Itasca State Park while he was a student at the Biological Station at Itasca. Aided by stuffed mammals and displays provided by the Bell Museum of Natural History in Minneapolis, he worked as a seasonal naturalist and then a volunteer from 1959 to 2004. He developed interpretive signs for many areas of the park and trail booklets and guides to the Dr. Roberts Trail (1960s) and Wilderness Drive (1985). His *Discover Itasca* and *Itasca Imponderables* series remain the cornerstones of the park's written materials and were later adapted by successive naturalists. Both series provide information to match the visitor's interest and background.

A FRIEND TO NATURE AND A HELPING HAND

Thoma advocated for natural preservation; as an example, he was involved in the 1987 decision that led to a halt of leech and minnow harvesting within the park and protected increasingly rare species. He was also noted for his quirky sense of humor. Lyle Colligan, a Clearwater County deputy sheriff who provided the first park security, recalls the day he stopped his patrol pickup and ran out to stop a car. The truck rolled back down a 50-yard incline and hit a huge tree, disabling the vehicle for some time. Next morning Lyle was greeted by a bicycle Ben had outfitted with a little bell and placard that said, "Park Patrol." Ben sometimes assisted Lyle in his duties, including a time that he helped "babysit some Hell's Angels" who arrived at the campground.

HISTORY SAVED FROM THE TRASH BIN

A dedicated collector, Ben "rescued" a houseful of documents, letters, photos, architects' drawings and other memorabilia from the discard bin and dump ground. His collection had boxes of random stuff, bureaucratic letters and the like, but it also included gems like the original architects' blueprints for the Forest Inn. He was able to farm most of this out to appropriate caretakers during his lifetime, and volunteers have spent countless hours cataloging and filing items of historical value. Current park naturalists Connie Cox and Sandra Lichter, aided during the summer by Naturalist Corps workers, run a robust lineup of programs for all ages and have been instrumental in developing interpretive displays for the new visitor centers and expanding children's programming.

REFINING THE TRAIL SYSTEM

Today's trail system is a compact version of the maze of trails and forest roads left behind by the CCC, early park builders and foresters. Ben Thoma, working with a crew on a Caterpillar and a brush hog, opened up and widened overgrown old trails so that they could be maintained and mowed with tractors and other power equipment. This has also proven essential for backcountry campsite development, skiing and firefighting. His 1965 report outlined the status of existing hiking trails and pointed out those that had fallen into disuse or were difficult to maintain. Based on that report, the staff closed trails, like the Blue Heron Trail connecting Nicollet and DeSoto, the Little Mantrap Trail that followed the historic 1883 wagon road from the southern border of the park west of Frazier Lake up to Iron Corner, and the Allen Lake Interpretive Trail near Aiton Heights Fire Tower. Thoma noted that most hikers on Bohall Trail would stop at the lake, so the park abandoned the rest of that trail, which once went all the way to the west shore of Lake Itasca. Other trails have changed too, including the LaSalle Trail, which used to lead from the University of Minnesota Biological Station all the way east to MN-200, and the Beaver Trail, which formerly wound through a tangle of spruce and balsam fir around LaSalle Springs but now has been rerouted to a short loop tucked into the northeast corner of the park. Though traces of these early trails remain, and some old forest roads even show up on modern online maps, they are difficult to follow and seldom used, except by a few deer hunters in the fall. The scaled-down trail system has been more efficient for the park to maintain and has allowed more of the park to return to its natural state.

Ozawindib Trail

CROSS-COUNTRY SKIERS HIT THE TRAILS

Cross-country skiers were welcomed to the park's trails in 1970. Some of the terrifying descents of those early days, like the hill on Deer Park Trail that featured a giant white pine at the bottom, have had their sharp downhill turns straightened or have become snowshoeing trails. Skate skiing lanes were added to some of the trails in the 1990s, when more skiers adopted this technique. Modern grooming equipment now works on the ski and snowmobile trails within the park, though grooming is still a challenge after deep snows blanket the remote, steep hills.

UPDATING THE BIKE TRAIL

Park resource managers have been studying routes for a redesigned bike trail from the Jacob V. Brower Visitor Center to the Headwaters for some time, as the trail had difficult corners and traverses archaeologically sensitive areas near Bear Paw Campground. They are rebuilding the middle of the trail, rerouting it east of Main Park Drive until it reaches the boat landing on Lake Itasca. The rest of the trail will be widened and resurfaced, with completion expected in 2014. Long-term plans include a connection from the Headwaters to the one-way section of Wilderness Drive and expanded connections to La Salle Lake State Recreation Area. A connection from the Heartland Trail near Park Rapids to the East Entrance of the park is also in the planning stage.

THE UNIVERSITY OF MINNESOTA AND ITASCA STATE PARK

The University of Minnesota Itasca Biological Station and Laboratories officially began its academic existence as the Itasca Summer School of Forestry in 1909, although a few students attended a summer session in 1908. Administered by the State Forestry Board at the time, Itasca State Park provided one of the first field study opportunities for forestry students. The station expanded its offerings to other biological sciences in 1954, and the broad-based biological research and education facility has served thousands of forestry and biology students over its 100-plus years. The Nature of Life summer experience gives incoming freshmen biology majors at the University of Minnesota a three-day intensive field and lab introduction to Itasca's ecosystems. The station has an extensive program of graduate and undergraduate research and academic courses. Though it is separate from Itasca State Park, the station has been a partner with the park administration in resource management over the years and has assisted with development of the Dr. Roberts Trail, wildlife management in the park, the park's controlled burning program and the establishment of the Wilderness Sanctuary National Landmark and Scientific Natural Area. The new campus center under construction will house updated research laboratories, an auditorium, classrooms, offices and a library.

CELEBRATING THE CENTENNIAL

Itasca celebrated its Centennial in 1991 by having 150 volunteers plant 17,000 pine seedlings in a single day. A Centennial Wagon Train, with Keith and Lynette Butler in the lead, joined the celebration, following the Mississippi River north from St. Paul. The group rolled into Itasca State Park with over 25 wagons and 200 volunteers. Riders and wagons on the 16-day trek followed ox-cart trails of the early pioneers whenever possible.

PLANS FOR THE FUTURE

Itasca State Park published a 200-page Comprehensive Management Plan in 1998, outlining the current state of the park, recommended changes, and its future mission. As a result, Itasca proceeded to build a new visitor center at the main park entrance. With the dedication of Jacob V. Brower Visitor Center in 2002, Itasca State Park has continued its tradition of grand buildings that carry on its mission of welcoming the public to the park and educating them about its cultural and natural history. Designed as a modern version of CCC architecture, the interior wood beams give it warmth that is truly a reflection of Itasca's past, and its spacious interior provides room to continually update interpretive displays and technology to keep up with future needs.

A BALANCING ACT

The park's 100-year mission statement called for "preservation and protection of the natural, historical, cultural and archaeological resources found within the park's boundaries while providing opportunities for park visitors to attain the experiences and benefits that they seek from recreational activities within the park." The plan clarified the uses of different areas of the park. A zone of concentrated use will exist on Main Park Drive and the more heavily used hiking trails near Douglas Lodge. The backcountry areas, which are lightly used, will provide opportunities for greater preservation of natural ecosystems. The Wilderness Sanctuary Scientific Natural Area will emphasize the preservation of natural systems with minimal human impact. Itasca's task for the future is to maintain this critical balance, so that future generations may continue to learn the lessons and experience the joys of a place that has delighted so many people in its first 120 years.

Recommended Reading and Resources

General

Minnesota Department of Natural Resources. "Itasca State Park." http://www.dnr.state.mn.us/state_parks/itasca/index.html

Minnesota Department of Natural Resources. "Itasca State Park Map and Guide" (available at visitor centers in the park)

Discover Itasca and *Itasca Imponderables* Series, a series of monographs by park naturalists and historians (available at the park)

Tester, John. *Minnesota's Natural Heritage: an Ecological Perspective.* Minneapolis: University of Minnesota Press, 1995.

History

Wingerd, Mary Lethert. *North Country: The Making of Minnesota.* Minneapolis: University of Minnesota Press, 2010.

Treuer, Anton. *Ojibwe in Minnesota (The People of Minnesota)* St. Paul: Minnesota Historical Society Press, 2010.

Vizenor, Gerald. *The People Named the Chippewa: Narrative Histories.* Minneapolis: University of Minnesota Press, 1984.

Warren, William. *History of the Ojibway People.* St. Paul: Minnesota Historical Society, 1885, 1984.

Brower, J. V. *The Mississippi River and its Source.* Minnesota Historical Society Collections (Vol. VII). Minneapolis: Harrison & Smith, State Printers, 1893. (available in libraries)

Brower, J. V. *Itasca State Park: An Illustrated History*, Minnesota Historical Collections, St. Paul, 1904. (available in libraries)

Bray, Martha Coleman (editor), and André Fertey (translator). *The Journals of Joseph N. Nicollet: A Scientist on the Mississippi Headwaters with Notes on Indian Life.* St. Paul: Minnesota Historical Society Press, 1970, 2004 reprint.

Dobie, John. *The Itasca Story.* Ross & Haines, 1959.

Cox, Connie, and Charlie Maguire. "Mary Gibbs: A Shining Light for Itasca." Minnesota Department of Natural Resources, Division of Parks and Trails. State Parks Files at the Minnesota Historical Society, 2008. (available at Itasca State Park)

Holland, Ren. *The Edge of Itasca: Life at Minnesota's Mississippi Headwaters and Early Itasca Park Communities.* The Book Lode, 2004.

Benson, David R. *Stories in Log and Stone: The Legacy of the New Deal in Minnesota State Parks.* State of Minnesota, Department of Natural Resources, 2002.

Harper, Mattie Marie. "French Africans in Ojibwe Country: Negotiating Marriage, Identity and Race, 1780–1890." UC Berkeley Electronic Theses and Dissertations, unpublished dissertation, p. 117, 2012. http://www.escholarship.org/uc/item/1zm0f6rt?query=harper,%20mattie%20marie (accessed 12/23/13)

Museums

Hubbard County Historical Museum, Park Rapids

Beltrami County History Center, Bemidji

Clearwater County History Center, Shevlin

Children

Louv, Richard. *Last Child in the Woods.* Algonquin Books, 2006.

Poppele, Jonathan. *Night Sky: A Field Guide to the Constellations.* Cambridge: Adventure Publications, 2009.

Poppele, Jonathan. *Animal Tracks: Midwest Edition.* Cambridge: Adventure Publications, 2012.

Porter, Adele. *Wild About Minnesota Birds*. Cambridge: Adventure Publications, 2007.

Wildlife Forever. *Critters of Minnesota Pocket Guide*. Cambridge: Adventure Publications, 2000.

Water Sports

Minnesota Department of Natural Resources. "Department of Natural Resources Aquatic Invasive Species – Programs, reports, and partners 2013." http://www.dnr.state.mn.us/invasives/aquatic_programs.html

Minnesota Department of Natural Resources. "2013 Boating Guide." http://files.dnr.state.mn.us/rlp/regulations/boatwater/boatingguide.pdf

Minnesota Department of Natural Resources. "2013 Fishing Regulations." http://files.dnr.state.mn.us/rlp/regulations/fishing/fishing2013.pdf

Minnesota Department of Natural Resources. "Mississippi River Water Trail Guide" (available at Brower Visitor Center or at http://www.dnr.state.mn.us/watertrails/mississippiriver/one.html)

Winter Sports

Note: Winter grooming reports for skiing and snowmobiling are available on Itasca State Park's website, by visiting or calling Brower Visitor Center. You can also check parkrapids.com, itascatur.org, or skinnyski.com

Minnesota Department of Natural Resources. "Ice Safety: When is Ice Safe?" http://www.dnr.state.mn.us/safety/ice/index.html

Trails

Hauser, Susan Carol (editor). *Guide to the North Country Trail in Minnesota*. Boulder: Big Earth Publishing, 2014.

Arthur, Anne. *Minnesota State Parks: How to Get There, What to Do, Where to Do It*. Cambridge: Adventure Publications, 2013.

Nature

Tekiela, Stan. *Mammals of Minnesota Field Guide*. Cambridge: Adventure Publications, 2005.

Hazard, Evan B. *The Mammals of Minnesota*. Minneapolis: University of Minnesota, 1982.

Tekiela, Stan. *Wildflowers of Minnesota Field Guide*. Cambridge: Adventure Publications, 1999.

Tekiela, Stan. *Trees of Minnesota Field Guide*. Cambridge: Adventure Publications, 2001.

"Minnesota Wildflowers." www.minnesotawildflowers.info

Newcomb, Lawrence. *Newcomb's Wildflower Guide*. New York City: Little, Brown and Co., 1977.

Peterson, Roger Tory, and Margaret McKenny. *Wildflowers Northeastern/North-central North America*. Boston: Houghton Mifflin Harcourt, 1996.

Risen, Kim, and Cindy Risen. *Orchids of the North Woods*. Duluth: Kollath+Stensaas Publishing, 2010.

Smith, Welby. *Trees and Shrubs of Minnesota*. Minneapolis: University of Minnesota Press, 2008.

Audubon Birds, iPad App.

Eckert, Kim R. *A Birder's Guide to Minnesota*. Plymouth: Williams Publications, Inc., 1994.

Tekiela, Stan. *Birds of Minnesota Field Guide (second edition)*. Cambridge: Adventure Publications, 2004.

References

Introduction

Snyder, Gary. *The Etiquette of Freedom: Gary Snyder, Jim Harrison and The Practice of the Wild*. New York City: North Point Press, 1990.

General References

Brower, J. V. *The Mississippi River and its Source*. Minnesota Historical Society Collections (Vol. VII). Minneapolis: Harrison & Smith, State Printers, 1893.

Brower, J. V. *Itasca State Park: An Illustrated History*. Minnesota Historical Collections (Vol. XI). St. Paul: Minnesota Historical Society, 1904.

Best of Itasca

Meuers, Michael. "Ojibwe/English words for everyday." Shared Vision Bemidji. http://www.sharedvisionbemidji.com/html/OjibweLanguage.pdf (accessed 5/31/13)

Wallace, Mrs. J. E. "Douglas Lodge Guest Book for the year 1921." St. Paul: Minnesota Historical Society Collections.

Biking

Minnesota Department of Transportation. "Mississippi River Trail (MRT) Bikeway Map Index." http://www.dot.state.mn.us/bike/mrt/maps/MRTmapsJune2011/Mapbook.pdf (accessed 4/11/13)

Visit Bemidji. "Biking Bemidji." http://www.visitbemidji.com/recreation/biking1.html (accessed 4/11/13)

Park Rapids Lakes Area Chamber of Commerce. "Biking and In-line Skating." http://parkrapids.com/biking.htm (accessed 4/11/13)

Minnesota Department of Natural Resources. "Paul Bunyan & Heartland State Trails." http://files.dnr.state.mn.us/maps/state_trails/paulbunyan_heartland.pdf (accessed 4/11/13)

Camping

Minnesota Department of Natural Resources. "Itasca State Park, Camping & Lodging." http://www.dnr.state.mn.us/state_parks/itasca/camping.html (accessed 3/1/13)

Minnesota Department of Natural Resources. "Reservations." http://www.dnr.state.mn.us/state_parks/reservations.html

Itasca with Children

American Academy of Pediatrics. "Safety and Prevention: Insect Repellents," 2013. http://www.healthychildren.org/English/safety-prevention/at-play/Pages/Insect-Repellents.aspx?nfstatus=401&nftoken=00000000-0000-0000-0000-000000000000&nfstatusdescription=ERROR%3a+No+local+token

Krautwurst, Terry. *Night Science for Kids, Exploring the World After Dark*. Asheville: Lark Books, 2003.

Louv, Richard. *Last Child in the Woods*. Chapel Hill: Algonquin Books, 2005.

Lodging

Evenwoll, Pat. "Bert's Cabins at Itasca State Park, Seventy Year History." 2009.

Evenwoll, Pat (personal communication, 4/18/13)

Minnesota Department of Natural Resources. "Itasca State Park." http://www.dnr.state.mn.us/state_parks/itasca/index.html (accessed 6/2/13)

Minnesota Department of Natural Resources. "Reservations." http://www.dnr.state.mn.us/state_parks/reservations.html

Minnesota Department of Natural Resources, Division of Parks and Trails. "Itasca State Park Historic Buildings and Structure Inventory." State Parks Files at the Minnesota Historical Society.

Planning Your Trip

Minnesota Department of Natural Resources. "Itasca State Park." http://www.dnr.state.mn.us/state_parks/itasca/index.html (accessed 6/2/13)

Weather.com. "Average Weather for Itasca State Park, MN – temperature and precipitation." http://www.weather.com/weather/wxclimatology/monthly/graph/6592:19 (accessed 2/27/13)

Tour of Itasca State Park—Scenic Drives, Sights, and Facilities

Minnesota Department of Natural Resources, Division of Parks and Trails. "Itasca State Park Map and Guide." State Parks Files at the Minnesota Historical Society.

Butler, Keith. "Itasca's Frontier Years." *Discover Itasca* Series (Vol. XIX). Minnesota Department of Natural Resources, Division of Parks and Trails. State Parks Files at the Minnesota Historical Society, 1996.

O'Sullivan, Thomas. "Indian Mounds—Minnesota Profile." *Minnesota Conservation Volunteer*. St. Paul: Minnesota Department of Natural Resources. March–April 2003. http://www.dnr.state.mn.us/volunteer/marapr03/mp-mounds.html (accessed 4/22/13)

Welle, Dorothy (personal communication, 4/30/13)

"Itasca Wilderness Sanctuary: Landscape of Beauty, Diversity, Solitude." *Discover Itasca* Series. Minnesota Department of Natural Resources, Division of Parks and Trails. State Parks Files at the Minnesota Historical Society.

Willett, Anita (personal communication)

Coburn, Jeannie (personal communication, 12/23/13)

Water Sports

Olson, Sigurd F. "The Way of a Canoe." *The Singing Wilderness*. New York: Knopf, 1955.

Minnesota Department of Natural Resources. "Guide to the Mississippi River: Minnesota State Water Trail Guide #1—Lake Itasca to Cass Lake." 2012

Minnesota Department of Natural Resources. "DNR Aquatic Invasive Species—Programs, reports, and partners 2013." http://www.dnr.state.mn.us/invasives/aquatic_programs.html (accessed 4/10/13)

Minnesota Department of Natural Resources. "2013 Boating Guide." http://files.dnr.state.mn.us/rlp/regulations/boatwater/boatingguide.pdf

Minnesota Department of Natural Resources. "2013 Fishing Regulations." http://files.dnr.state.mn.us/rlp/regulations/fishing/fishing2013.pdf

Winter Sports in Itasca

Minnesota Department of Natural Resources. "Ice Safety: When is Ice Safe?" http://www.dnr.state.mn.us/safety/ice/index.html (accessed 2/2/13)

Cass County, Minnesota. "Ski Trail Maps." http://www.co.cass.mn.us/maps/map_trails.html

Snowmobiling

Kimball, Richard (personal communication, 11/22/13)

Ohm, Richard (personal communication, 9/14/13)

Driving Tour of Itasca

"Scenic Drive Built Around Lake Itasca." *Park Rapids Enterprise*, 7/30/25.

Hiking Trail Guide: General References to Names, Including Trail Names

"Itasca's Trails." *Discover Itasca* Series (Vol. VIII). Minnesota Department of Natural Resources, Division of Parks and Trails. State Parks Files at the Minnesota Historical Society.

Upham, Warren. *Minnesota's Geographic Names: Their Origin and Historic Significance*. St. Paul: Minnesota Historical Society, 1969.

Genealogy Trails 2012, "Itasca Place Names and genealogy." http://genealogytrails.com/minn/clearwater/history_countynames.html (accessed 10/5/12)

North Country National Scenic Trail

Hauser, Susan Carol (editor). *Guide to the North Country Trail in Minnesota*. Boulder: Big Earth Publishing, 2014.

Aiton Heights

Thoma, Ben. "The History of the Aiton Fire Tower." http://www.paulbunyan.net/itasca/index_files/Page412.htm (accessed 3/13/13)

Minnesota Department of Natural Resources, Division of Parks and Trails. State Parks Files at the Minnesota Historical Society.

Bachman, Elizabeth. "Honorable Order of Squirrels." Minnesota Division of Forestry. http://webapps8.dnr. state.mn.us/mcv_pdf/012_072/012_072_Text/0051.txt (accessed 3/13/13)

Big White Pine Trail and Big Red Pine/Bison Kill Site Trail

Shay, C. Thomas. *The Itasca Bison Kill Site: An Ecological Analysis*. St. Paul: Minnesota Historical Society, 1971.

Bohall Trail and Brower Trail

Spurr, Stephen H. "Forest Fire History of Itasca State Park." *Minnesota Forestry Notes No. 18*, University of Minnesota School of Forestry and the Minnesota Conservation Department Division of Forestry, 6/15/1955.

Gentry, C., et al. "Reanalysis of the Fire History in *Pinus resinosa* stands of the Mississippi Headwaters, Itasca State Park, Minnesota." Current research colloquia poster, Dendrochronology Lab, Indiana State University, 2005. http://dendrolab.indstate.edu/old%20website%20files/curr_research/colloquia_poster. pdf (accessed 12/17/13)

CCC Forestry Demonstration Area

"In Their Words: Stories of Minnesota's Greatest Generation." *The Civilian Conservation Corps Experience*. St. Paul: Minnesota Historical Society. http://stories.mnhs.org/stories/mgg/scene.do?id=2 (accessed 3/14/13)

DeSoto Trail (and History: Early Mississippi Explorers)

Brower, J. V. *Itasca State Park: An Illustrated History*. Minnesota Historical Collections (Vol. XI). St. Paul: Minnesota Historical Society, 1904.

Wikipedia, The Free Encyclopedia. "Hernando de Soto." http://en.wikipedia.org/wiki/Hernando_de_Soto (accessed 10/1/12)

Wikipedia, The Free Encyclopedia. "Alonso Álvarez de Pineda." http://en.wikipedia.org/wiki/Alonso_Álvarez_de_Pineda (accessed 10/1/12).

Atkins, Leah Rawls, et al. "European Exploration and Colonization in Alabama." *Alabama: The History of a Deep South State*. Tuscaloosa, Alabama: University of Alabama Press, 1994.

Morison, Samuel. *The European Discovery of America: The Southern Voyages, 1492–1616*. New York: Oxford University Press, 1974.

Wikipedia, The Free Encyclopedia. "Antoine Auguelle." http://en.wikipedia.org/wiki/Antoine_Auguelle (accessed 11/12/12)

Dr. Roberts Trail

Itasca State Park staff. "Dr. Roberts Nature Trail." Minnesota Department of Natural Resources, Division of Parks and Trails. State Parks Files at the Minnesota Historical Society.

East Entrance CCC Section Corner

Thoma, Ben. *Itasca Imponderables* Series (Vol. V). Minnesota Department of Natural Resources, Division of Parks and Trails. State Parks Files at the Minnesota Historical Society.

Headwaters Trails

Thoma, Ben. "The Mississippi Headwaters" *Itasca Imponderables* Series, Minnesota Department of Natural Resources, Division of Parks and Trails. State Parks Files at the Minnesota Historical Society.

Mary Lake Trail and Deer Exclosure

Ross, Bruce A., and J. Roger Bray and William H. Marshall. "Effects of Long-term Deer Exclusion on a *Pinus resinosa* Forest in North-central Minnesota." *Ecology*, Vol. 51, No. 6, November 1970.

Eagle Scout-North Country Trail

Dobie, John. *The Itasca Story*. Ross & Haines, 1959.

North Country NST— Hiking near Itasca

"North Country National Scenic Trail." Minnesota Department of Natural Resources, Division of Parks and Trails. State Parks Files at the Minnesota Historical Society.

North Country Trail (NCT)—DeSoto to Morrison

Brower, J. V. *The Mississippi River and its Source*. Minnesota Historical Society Collections (Vol. VII). Minneapolis: Harrison & Smith, State Printers, 1893.

North Country Trail—Morrison to West Boundary

North Country Trail Association. "Maps and online information." http://northcountrytrail.org/trail/states/minnesota/explore-by-section/laurentian-lakes-chapter/trail-description/ (accessed 4/29/13)

Vlasak, Ray (personal communication, 4/29/13)

Sawmill Trail

Hemmerich, Leonard (personal communication, 5/31/13)

Schoolcraft Trail

Smith, Welby. *Trees and Shrubs of Minnesota*. Minneapolis: University of Minnesota Press, 2008.

Natural History: Shaping the Landscape

Thoma, Ben (editor). "Generalized lithologic log from MGS Hole HB-87-1." *Itasca State Park Centennial: Itasca Imponderables* Series. Minnesota Department of Natural Resources, Division of Parks and Trails. State Parks Files at the Minnesota Historical Society.

Zumberge, James H. "Geology of Itasca State Park." *Minnesota Conservation Volunteer*, November/December 1952.

"Ice and Water Sculpt the Landscape of Itasca State Park." *Discover Itasca* Series (Vol. VIII). Minnesota Department of Natural Resources, Division of Parks and Trails. State Parks Files at the Minnesota Historical Society.

Minnesota Department of Natural Resources, Division of Parks and Trails. "Itasca State Park Management Plan, December 1998." State Parks Files at the Minnesota Historical Society.

Ojakangas, Richard W. *Roadside Geology of Minnesota*. Missoula: Mountain Press Publishing Company, 2009.

Tester, John R. *Minnesota's Natural Heritage: An Ecological Perspective*. Minneapolis: University of Minnesota Press, 1995.

Parson, Charlie. "Rip, Flow, and Ice—Geology of the North Woods." Master Naturalist Syllabus (Draft). Minneapolis: University of Minnesota, 2011.

Trees

Miller, Kerri, and Paul Huttner. "Climate Change Expected to Hit Minnesota with Rising Temps." Minnesota Public Radio, 1/17/2013. www.mpr.org (accessed 1/29/13)

Smith, Welby. *Trees and Shrubs of Minnesota*. Minnesota Department of Natural Resources. Minneapolis: University of Minnesota Press, 2008.

Tester, John R. *Minnesota's Natural Heritage: An Ecological Perspective*. Minneapolis: University of Minnesota Press, 1995.

Hughes, Judy. "The Magnificent Pines." *Discover Itasca* Series (Vol. V). Minnesota Department of Natural Resources, Division of Parks and Trails. State Parks Files at the Minnesota Historical Society.

Bradbury, J. Platt, and Dean, Walter E. (eds.). *Elk Lake, Minnesota: Evidence for Rapid Climate Change in the North-Central United States*. Boulder: Geologic Society of America, 1993.

Tjader, Harvey. "Forestry Management and Climate Change." (lecture, 10/5/13)

Wikipedia, The Free Encyclopedia. "Pando (tree)." http://en.wikipedia.org/wiki/Pando_(tree) (accessed 5/8/13)

Mammals

"Elk encounter." *Park Rapids Enterprise*, 12/25/30.

West, Mrs. Jessie C. *A Pioneer History of Becker County, Minnesota*. St. Paul: Pioneer Press Company, 1907.

Tester, John. "The Beaver in Itasca." *Discover Itasca* Series (Vol. XI). Minnesota Department of Natural Resources, Division of Parks and Trails. State Parks Files at the Minnesota Historical Society.

Hazard, Evan B. *The Mammals of Minnesota*. Minneapolis: University of Minnesota Press, 1982.

Tekiela, Stan. *Mammals of Minnesota Field Guide*. Cambridge: Adventure Publications, 2005.

"Deer and Itasca." *Discover Itasca* Series (Vol. XXIII). Minnesota Department of Natural Resources, Division of Parks and Trails. State Parks Files at the Minnesota Historical Society.

"Beaver." *Park Rapids Enterprise*, 5/2/18.

Bats

Science Daily. "Fewer Bats Carry Rabies Than Thought," 3/22/11. http://www.sciencedaily.com/releases/2011/01/110131133323.htm (accessed 12/13/12)

Minnesota Department of Heath. "Management of Human-Bat Encounters." http://www.health.state.mn.us/divs/idepc/diseases/rabies/risk/humanbat.html (accessed 12/13/12)

Menken, Jennifer. "Bats in Houses." University of Minnesota Extension. http://www.extension.umn.edu/distribution/horticulture/M1281.html (accessed 12/13/12)

Bobcats

Hansen, Kevin. *Bobcat: Master of Survival*. Oxford: Oxford University Press, 2007.

West, Mrs. Jessie C., and Alvin Wilcox. *A Pioneer History of Becker County Minnesota, including a brief account of its natural history*. St. Paul: Pioneer Press Company, 1907.

Birds

Minnesota Department of Natural Resources, Division of Parks and Trails. "Itasca State Park bird checklist." http://files.dnr.state.mn.us/destinations/state_parks/itasca/bird_checklist.pdf (accessed 4/24/13)

Howe, Marshall (personal communication, 4/24/13, 5/6/13)

Audubon Birds. iPad App. (accessed 4/25/13)

Eckert, Kim R. *A Birder's Guide to Minnesota*. Plymouth: Williams Publications, Inc., 1994.

Tekiela, Stan. *Birds of Minnesota Field Guide (second edition)*. Cambridge: Adventure Publications, 2004.

Green, Janet C. *Birds and Forests, A Management and Conservation Guide*. St. Paul: Minnesota Department of Natural Resources, 1995.

Dickson, Tom. "Why Do Grouse Boom and Bust?" *Minnesota Conservation Volunteer*, November/December 2006.

Erickson, Laura. *Sharing the Wonder of Birds With Kids*. Duluth: Pfeifer-Hamilton, 1997.

Butterflies

Weber, Larry. *Butterflies of the North Woods: Minnesota, Wisconsin, & Michigan, 2nd Edition*. Duluth: Kollath+Stensaas Publishing, 2006.

Weber, John (personal communication, 12/10/13)

Amphibians and Reptiles

Minnesota Department of Natural Resources. "Reptiles/Amphibians of Minnesota." http://www.dnr.state.mn.us/reptiles_amphibians/index.html

Wildflowers

"Minnesota Wildflowers." www.minnesotawildflowers.info

Newcomb, Lawrence. *Newcomb's Wildflower Guide*. New York City: Little, Brown and Co., 1977.

Peterson, Roger Tory, and Margaret McKenny. *Wildflowers Northeastern/North-central North America*. Boston: Houghton Mifflin Harcourt, 1996.

Tekiela, Stan. *Wildflowers of Minnesota Field Guide.* Cambridge: Adventure Publications, 1999.

Risen, Kim, and Cindy Risen. *Orchids of the North Woods.* Duluth: Kollath+Stensaas Publishing, 2010.

La Salle Lake State Recreation Area (SRA) and Scientific Natural Area (SNA)

Minnesota Department of Natural Resources. "La Salle State Recreation Area Fact Sheet." http://files.dnr.state.mn.us/input/mgmtplans/parks/lasalle/lasalle_factsheet.pdf

Weir-Koetter, Chris (personal communication, 9/18/13, 12/16/13)

Gronewold, Chris (email, 9/17/13)

Smith, Welby. *Orchids of Minnesota.* Minnesota Department of Natural Resources. Minneapolis: University of Minnesota Press, 1993.

History References

General References

Brower, J. V. *The Mississippi River and its Source.* Minnesota Historical Society Collections (Vol. VII). Minneapolis: Harrison & Smith, State Printers, 1893.

Brower, J. V. *Itasca State Park: An Illustrated History,* Minnesota Historical Collections (Vol. XI). St. Paul: Minnesota Historical Society Press, 1904.

Dobie, John. *The Itasca Story.* Ross & Haines, 1959.

Wingerd, Mary Lethert. *North Country: The Making of Minnesota.* Minneapolis: University of Minnesota Press, 2010.

Indigenous People of the Itasca State Park Region

White Earth Reservation Curriculum Committee. *White Earth: A History.* Cass Lake: Minnesota Chippewa Tribe, 1989.

Treuer, Anton. *Ojibwe in Minnesota (The People of Minnesota).* St. Paul: Minnesota Historical Society Press, 2010.

Treuer, Anton. *The Assassination of Hole in the Day.* Borealis Books, St. Paul: Minnesota Historical Society Press, 2011.

Vizenor, Gerald. *The People Named the Chippewa: Narrative Histories.* Minneapolis: University of Minnesota Press, 1984.

Warren, William. *History of the Ojibway People.* St. Paul: Minnesota Historical Society Press, 1885, 1984.

White Earth Nation. "History." http://www.whiteearth.com/history/ (accessed 12/30/12)

From Site to Story, The Institute for Minnesota Archaeology. "Mississippi River From Site to Story: The Upper Mississippi's Buried Past." http://www.fromsitetostory.org/stories.asp (accessed 12/30/12, 1/3/13)

From Site to Story, The Institute for Minnesota Archaeology. "Itasca Bison Kill Site." http://www.fromsitetostory.org/stories.asp (accessed 12/30/12, 1/3/13)

From Site to Story, The Institute for Minnesota Archaeology. "Pamida Burial Salvage Project." http://www.fromsitetostory.org/stories.asp (accessed 12/30/12, 1/3/13)

From Site to Story, The Institute for Minnesota Archaeology. "LaSalle Creek." http://www.fromsitetostory.org/stories.asp (accessed 12/30/12, 1/3/13)

From Site to Story, The Institute for Minnesota Archaeology. "Necktie River." http://www.fromsitetostory.org/stories.asp (accessed 12/30/12, 1/3/13)

Gilman, Rhoda R. *The Story of Minnesota's Past.* St. Paul: Minnesota Historical Society Press, 1989, 1991.

Wub-e-ke-niew, *We Have the Right to Exist: A Translation of Aboriginal Indigenous Thought.* New York: Black Thistle Press, New York, 1995.

Arzigian, Constance M., and Katherine P. Stevenson. *Minnesota's Indian Mounds and Burial Sites: A Synthesis of Prehistoric and Early Historic Archaeological Data.* St. Paul: Minnesota Office of the State Archaeologist, 2003.

Park Naturalist Staff. "Itasca's Prehistoric Heritage." *Discover Itasca* Series. Minnesota Department of Natural Resources, Division of Parks and Trails. State Parks Files at the Minnesota Historical Society.

Shay, C. Thomas. *The Itasca Bison Kill Site: An Ecological Analysis*. St. Paul: Minnesota Historical Society Press, 1971.

Gibbon, Guy E. *Archaeology of Minnesota: The Prehistory of the Upper Mississippi River Region*. Minneapolis: University of Minnesota Press, 2012.

Early Mississippi Explorers: De Soto, La Salle, Hennepin, Du Luth, Pike, Cass, Beltrami

Brower, J. V. *The Mississippi River and its Source*. Minnesota Historical Society Collections (Vol. VII). Minneapolis: Harrison & Smith, State Printers, 1893.

Flutopedia. "The Beltrami Flutes—The earliest known Native American Flute." http://www.flutopedia.com/beltrami.htm (accessed 1/3/13)

Wikipedia, The Free Encyclopedia. "Hernando de Soto." http://en.wikipedia.org/wiki/Hernando_de_Soto (accessed 1/3/13)

Wingerd, Mary Lethert. *North Country: The Making of Minnesota*. Minneapolis: University of Minnesota, 2010.

Parkman, Francis. *France and England in North America: La Salle and the discovery of the Great West*. New York: Little, Brown, 1892, 1902.

De Tonty, Henri, and Melville B. Anderson (translator). *Relation of Henri De Tonty Concerning the Explorations of La Salle*. Chicago: The Caxton Club, 1898.

Hall, Steven P. *Itasca: Source of America's Greatest River*. St. Paul: Minnesota Historical Society, 1982.

Hall, Steve. "Charting Lake Itasca." *Discover Itasca* Series (Vol. IV). Minnesota Department of Natural Resources, Division of Parks and Trails. State Parks Files at the Minnesota Historical Society.

Pike, Z. M., and Elliot Coues. *The Expeditions of Zebulon Montgomery Pike: to the Headwaters of the Mississippi River etc*. New York: F. P. Harper, 1895.

William Morrison

Brower, J. V. *The Mississippi River and its Source*. Minnesota Historical Society Collections (Vol. VII). Minneapolis: Harrison & Smith, State Printers, 1893.

Mellor, Bruce. "William Morrison—Fur Trader, 1994." Morrison County Historical Society. http://morrison-countyhistory.org/history/?page_id=404 (accessed 1/3/13)

Schoolcraft's Expedition

Mason, Philip P. (editor) *Schoolcraft's Expedition to Lake Itasca*. East Lansing: Michigan State University Press, Michigan, 1958.

Brower, J. V. *The Mississippi River and its Source*. Minnesota Historical Society Collections (Vol. VII). Minneapolis: Harrison & Smith, State Printers, 1893.

Petersen, William J. "Veritas Caput Itasca" in Notes and Documents, *Minnesota History Magazine* (Vol. XVIII). http://collections.mnhs.org/mnhistorymagazine/articles/18/v18i02p180-185.pdf (accessed 5/3/13)

Gale, Edward C. "Itasca Studies: The Legend of Lake Itasca." St. Paul: Minnesota Historical Society.

The Lawrence Taliaferro Papers. St. Paul: Minnesota Historical Society.

Folwell, William Watts. *A History of Minnesota*. St. Paul: Minnesota Historical Society Press, 1922.

Joseph N. Nicollet

Bray, Martha Coleman (editor), and André Fertey (translator). *The Journals of Joseph N. Nicollet: A Scientist on the Mississippi Headwaters With Notes on Indian Life*. St. Paul: Minnesota Historical Society, 1970.

Brower, J. V. *The Mississippi River and its Source*. Minnesota Historical Society Collections (Vol. VII). Minneapolis: Harrison & Smith, State Printers, 1893.

Nicollet, J. N. "Report Intended to Illustrate a Map of the Hydrographical Basin of the Upper Mississippi River." U. S. Senate Report, 26th Congress, 2nd Session, February 16, 1841. Washington: Blair and Rives Printers, 1843. (accessed 12/22/13)

Julius T. Chambers

Chambers, Julius T. *The Mississippi River and its Wonderful Valley.* New York and London: G. P. Putnam's Sons, 1910.

Brower, J. V. *The Mississippi River and its Source.* Minnesota Historical Society Collections (Vol. VII). Minneapolis: Harrison & Smith, State Printers, 1893.

"The Glazier Fiasco"

Glazier, Willard. *Down the Great River: Embracing an Account of the Discovery of the True Source of the Mississippi.* Philadelphia, 1887.

Glazier, Willard. *Headwaters of the Mississippi; Comprising biographical sketches of early and recent explorers of the great river, and a full account of the discovery and location of its true source in a lake beyond Itasca.* Chicago and New York: Rand, McNally & Company, 1893.

Henderson, Connie. "The Naming of Hubbard County Townships, Part Two." Hubbard County Historical Museum. http://hubbardcountyhistoricalmuseum.areavoices.com/2012/01/19/ (accessed 10/7/12)

Brower, J. V. *Itasca State Park: An Illustrated History.* Minnesota Historical Collections (Vol. XI). St. Paul: Minnesota Historical Society Press, 1904.

Brower, J. V. *The Mississippi River and its Source.* Minnesota Historical Society Collections (Vol. VII). Minneapolis: Harrison & Smith, State Printers, 1893.

Dobie, John. *The Itasca Story.* Ross & Haines, 1959.

Surveyors and Visitors

Baker, James H. "The Sources of the Mississippi. Their discoverers, real and pretended." Minnesota Historical Collection (Vol. VI, part I). St. Paul: Minnesota Historical Society, 1887.

Wikipedia, The Free Encyclopedia. "Henry Benjamin Whipple." http://en.wikipedia.org/wiki/Henry_Benjamin_Whipple (accessed 1/11/13)

Clarke, Hopewell. "The Source of the Mississippi." *Science,* (Vol. VIII), 12/24/1886.

MNOPEDIA, Minnesota Encyclopedia. "Bonga, George (1802–1880)." http://www.mnopedia.org/person/bonga-george-1802-1880 (accessed 1/11/13)

Brower, J. V. *The Mississippi River and its Source.* Minnesota Historical Society Collections (Vol. VII). Minneapolis: Harrison & Smith, State Printers, 1893.

The Fight for Itasca State Park

Llewellyn, C. L., and J. V. Brower. "The fight for Itasca Park: J.V. Brower's long struggle and unselfish devotion to save to Minnesota this gift of nature." *Western Magazine,* Vol. 17(5), pp. 146–152, 1922.

Brower, J. V., *Itasca State Park: An Illustrated History,* Minnesota Historical Collections (Vol. XI). St. Paul: Minnesota Historical Society, 1904.

Brower, J. V. *The Mississippi River and its Source.* Minnesota Historical Society Collections (Vol. VII). Minneapolis: Harrison & Smith, State Printers, 1893.

Dobie, John. *The Itasca Story.* Ross & Haines, 1959.

Hall, Steve. "Birth of the Park." *Discover Itasca* Series (Vol. X). Minnesota Department of Natural Resources, Division of Parks and Trails. State Parks Files at the Minnesota Historical Society.

Cox, Connie. "Douglas Lodge: Minnesota's Own Resort." Minnesota Department of Natural Resources, Division of Parks and Trails. State Parks Files at the Minnesota Historical Society.

Hubbard County Enterprise, 3/31/1904, 6/29/1905, 7/6/1905.

Butler, Keith. "Itasca's Frontier Years." *Discover Itasca* Series (Vol. XIX). Minnesota Department of Natural Resources, Division of Parks and Trails. State Parks Files at the Minnesota Historical Society, 1996.

Gimmestad, Dennis, et al. "Itasca State Park's Rustic Style Log Buildings." *Discover Itasca* Series (Vol. XII). Minnesota Department of Natural Resources, Division of Parks and Trails. State Parks Files at the Minnesota Historical Society.

"A lot of work kept Itasca resort thriving for 70 years." *Farmers Independent*. Bagley, Minnesota, 1/6/10. http://smalltownnews.com/article.php?catname=Business&pub=Farmers%20Independent&pid=188&aid=702 (accessed 2/26/13)

Vandersluis, Charles, et al. "Mainly Logging: A Compilation." Minneota Clinic, 1974.

Cox, Connie, and Charlie Maguire. "Mary Gibbs: A Shining Light for Itasca." Minnesota Department of Natural Resources, Division of Parks and Trails. State Parks Files at the Minnesota Historical Society, 2008.

Maguire, Charlie. "She Freed the Mississippi." *Discover Itasca* Series (Vol. XVI). Minnesota Department of Natural Resources, Division of Parks and Trails. State Parks Files at the Minnesota Historical Society.

Early Settlers

Brower, J. V. *The Mississippi River and its Source*. Minnesota Historical Society Collections (Vol. VII.) Minneapolis: Harrison & Smith, State Printers, 1893.

"Killed for a Deer!" *Park Rapids Enterprise,* 11/4/1898.

Butler, Keith. "Itasca's Frontier Years." *Discover Itasca* Series (Vol. XIX). Minnesota Department of Natural Resources, Division of Parks and Trails. State Parks Files at the Minnesota Historical Society.

"Mrs. Henselman . . . Lynx." *Akeley Tribune*, 3/21/1907.

"Theodore Wegmann, 79." *Park Rapids Enterprise*, 7/3/41.

Park Rapids Enterprise, several articles from 1921.

Holland, Ren. *The Edge of Itasca: Life at Minnesota's Mississippi Headwaters and Early Itasca Park Communities*. The Book Lode, 2004.

Mitchell, Frank (personal communication, 3/28/13)

Dobie, John. *The Itasca Story*. Ross & Haines, 1959.

Jefferson Highway

Mitchell, Frank. "Park Rapids, Itasca Park, and the Jefferson Highway" (manuscript), 2013.

Mitchell, Frank (personal communication, 3/28/13)

Brower, J. V. *Itasca State Park: An Illustrated History*. Minnesota Historical Collections (Vol. XI). St. Paul: Minnesota Historical Society, 1904.

"Jefferson Highway Sociability Run." *Park Rapids Enterprise*, 8/16/16.

"Jefferson Highway Association." www.jeffersonhighway.org (accessed 3/7/13)

Holland, Ren (personal communication, 5/28/13)

"Sociability Jefferson Highway Run." *Park Rapids Enterprise*, 5/17/17, 5/29/19.

"200 Tourists Coming on Sociability Trip." *Park Rapids Enterprise*, 7/9/25.

Civilian Conservation Corps in Itasca

Benson, David R. *Stories in Log and Stone: The Legacy of the New Deal in Minnesota State Parks*. St. Paul: Minnesota Department of Natural Resources, 2002.

Thoma, Ben. "The Civilian Conservation Corps and Itasca State Park." *Discover Itasca* Series (Vol. XIV). Minnesota Department of Natural Resources, Division of Parks and Trails. State Parks Files at the Minnesota Historical Society.

Thoma, Ben. "The Mississippi Headwaters." *Itasca Imponderables* Series (Vol. II). Minnesota Department of Natural Resources, Division of Parks and Trails. State Parks Files at the Minnesota Historical Society.

Czeczok, Leroy, and Louise Czeczok, Murl McGrane and Kathy McGrane (personal communication, 10/30/12)

"Itasca State Park Historic Buildings and Structure Inventory." Minnesota Department of Natural Resources, Division of Parks and Trails. State Parks Files at the Minnesota Historical Society.

Sommer, Barbara W. *Hard Work and a Good Deal: The Civilian Conservation Corps in Minnesota*. St. Paul: Minnesota Historical Society Press, 2008.

Thoma, Ben. "The Civilian Conservation Corps and Itasca State Park." Minnesota Department of Natural Resources, Division of Parks and Trails. State Parks Files at the Minnesota Historical Society, 1984.

Farmers Independent, 10/24/35.

"Itasca State Park: National Register listing, May 1992 update." Minnesota Department of Natural Resources, Division of Parks and Trails. State Parks Files at the Minnesota Historical Society. http://www.mnhs.org/places/nationalregister/stateparks/Itasca.html (accessed 9/8/13)

Tschudi, Don (personal communication, 5/28/13)

"Various CCC news items." *Park Rapids Enterprise*, 10/7/37, 3/24/38, 3/31/38.

"Scenic Drive Built Around Lake Itasca." *Park Rapids Enterprise*, 7/30/25.

The Itasca Pageants 1932–1938

Bilden, Bob A. "75 Years pass since first Schoolcraft centennial pageant at Itasca." *Farmers Independent*, 7/11/2007.

"The Historical Pageants, interpretive plaque, Itasca State Park." Minnesota Department of Natural Resources, Division of Parks and Trails. State Parks Files at the Minnesota Historical Society.

Van Koughnet, Donald. *The State Historical Convention of 1932*. St. Paul: Minnesota Historical Society, 1932.

Mitchell, Frank. "Historical Pageants—Itasca State Park," *Byway Buzz*. Minnesota Scenic Byway, 2005.

Mitchell, Frank (personal communication, 3/28/13)

Conzet, Grover. "The Historical Pageants Presented at Itasca State Park, 1932–1933." Minnesota Department of Natural Resources, Division of Parks and Trails. State Parks Files at the Minnesota Historical Society.

Willard, E. V. "The Historical Pageants presented at Itasca State park 1932–1933." Minnesota Department of Conservation. Northwestern Minnesota Historical Association.

Schrum, Lloyd (personal communication, 11/14/13)

Park Buildings and Development

"National Register of Historic Places/State Parks." State Parks Files at the Minnesota Historical Society. http://www.mnhs.org/places/nationalregister/stateparks/Itasca.html (accessed 2/27/13)

Llewellyn, C. L., and J. V. Brower. "The Fight for Itasca Park: J.V. Brower's Long Struggle and Unselfish Devotion to Save to Minnesota This Gift of Nature." *Western Magazine*, Vol. 17(5), 1922.

Brower, J. V. *Itasca State Park: An Illustrated History*. Minnesota Historical Collections (Vol. XI). St. Paul: Minnesota Historical Society, 1904.

Brower, J. V. *The Mississippi River and its Source*. Minnesota Historical Society Collections (Vol. VII). Minneapolis: Harrison & Smith, State Printers, 1893.

Hall, Steve. "Birth of the Park." *Discover Itasca* Series (Vol. X). Minnesota Department of Natural Resources, Division of Parks and Trails. State Parks Files at the Minnesota Historical Society.

Cox, Connie. *Douglas Lodge: Minnesota's Own Resort*. Itasca State Park, Minnesota Department of Natural Resources, Division of Parks and Trails. State Parks Files at the Minnesota Historical Society.

Cox, Connie (personal communication, 5/9/13)

Hubbard County Enterprise, 3/31/1904, 6/29/1905, 7/6/1905.

Butler, Keith. "Itasca's Frontier Years." *Discover Itasca* Series (Vol. XIX). Minnesota Department of Natural Resources, Division of Parks and Trails. State Parks Files at the Minnesota Historical Society, 1996.

Gimmestad, Dennis, et al. "Itasca State Park's Rustic Style Log Buildings." *Discover Itasca* Series (Vol. XII). Minnesota Department of Natural Resources, Division of Parks and Trails. State Parks Files at the Minnesota Historical Society.

"Killed for a Deer!" *Park Rapids Enterprise*, 11/4/1898.

"A lot of work kept Itasca resort thriving for 70 years." *Farmers Independent* staff, 1/6/10. http://small townnews.com/article.php?catname=Business&pub=Farmers%20Independent&pid=188&aid=702 (accessed 2/26/2013)

Vandersluis, Charles, et al. *Mainly Logging: A Compilation*. Minneota Clinic, 1974.

Cox, Connie, and Charlie Maguire. "Mary Gibbs: A Shining Light for Itasca." Minnesota Department of Natural Resources, Division of Parks and Trails. State Parks Files at the Minnesota Historical Society, 2008.

The Modern Era

Thoma, Ben. "Letter to Bonnie Wilson." Minnesota Historical Society, 4/30/2003. Minnesota Department of Natural Resources, Division of Parks and Trails. State Parks Files at the Minnesota Historical Society.

Vojak, Lorraine (personal communication, 7/24/13)

Rieger, Amy K. and Ben Thoma. "Itasca State Park Oral History Project, 06/23/1993–8/31/2000." Minnesota Historical Society and the Minnesota Department of Natural Resources (dates noted for individual references)
    Keith Butler, with Amy Rieger (7/29/93)
    Bert Pfeifer, with Amy Rieger (7/20/93 and 8/20/93)
    Alvin and Dorothy Katzenmeyer with Ben Thoma (7/20/00)
    Reuben Law with Amy Rieger , Ben Thoma, Ron Miles (6/23/93)
    Elon and Alma Cary with Amy Rieger (9/14/93)
    Myrtie Hunt with Amy Rieger (8/5/93)
    Lyle Colligan with Ben Thoma (8/30/00)

Colligan, Lyle (personal communication, 9/11/13)

Thoma, Bill (personal communication, 9/11/13)

Itasca State Park Management Plan, December 1998. Minnesota Department of Natural Resources, Division of Parks and Trails. State Parks Files at the Minnesota Historical Society.

"William Butler Obituary." *Farmers Independent*, 02/08/06.

Sawyer, Darlene. "Church stays open in summers." *Farmers Independent*, 09/15/10.

Thoma, Ben. "1965 Itasca State Park Trail Inventory and Report." Minnesota Department of Natural Resources, Division of Parks and Trails. State Parks Files at the Minnesota Historical Society.

Thoma, Ben. "Letter to Bonnie Wilson re: Ben Littlecreek 4/30/03." Minnesota Department of Natural Resources, Division of Parks and Trails. State Parks Files at the Minnesota Historical Society.

Thoma, Bill (personal communication, email, 9/11/13) [Brett, Bill Thoma is already listed above for this date, after Colligan, after the indented list]

Evenwoll, Pat (personal communication, 7/29/13)

Katzenmeyer, Dorothy (personal communication, 10/7/13)

Katzenmeyer, Jack (personal communication, 9/30/13)

Sauer, Dick (personal communication, 12/1/13)

Colligan, Lyle (personal communication, 9/13/13)

Rubenstein, Doris (editor). *Itasca at 90: A History in Memories*. College of Biological Sciences. Minneapolis: University of Minnesota, 1999.

Fider, Erin (personal communication, 7/29/13)

"Itasca Traditions: Tourism 1930s to present" (brochure). Minnesota Department of Natural Resources, Division of Parks and Trails. State Parks Files at the Minnesota Historical Society.

"Nicollet Cabin." *Minnesota Cities*, Vol. 80, No. 12, December 1995.

Photo Credits

162 Trista Little (Dr. Roberts Trail). **164** Paul Peterson (Skijoring). **193** "At the Source of the Father of Waters," 1932-1933 Pageant Book by the Northwest Minnesota Historical Association, courtesy of Hubbard County Historical Museum. **194** Dale Sheldon and Brita Sailer (bison). **198** Public domain image of a painting of Father Hennepin, circa 1683. **211** Hubbard County Historical Museum. **222** Beltrami County Historical Society (BCHS-41). **223** Beltrami County Historical Society (BCHS-20). **224** Collection Photo—Clearwater County Historical Society. **226** Clearwater County Historical Society. **230** Clearwater County Historical Society. **233** Connie and Gene Henderson (from the Marvin Henderson Collection). **237** Hubbard County Historical Museum and the *Park Rapids Enterprise's* book, *Hubbard County: A Century of Growth, 1900–2000*. **239** "At the Source of the Father of Waters," Hubbard County Historical Museum. **245** (Mizpah Survey Crew) Beltrami County Historical Society (BCHS-1760). **272** Trista Little (author photo).

The photos on the following pages originate from Jacob V. Brower's *The Mississippi River and Its Source*. Minnesota Historical Society Collections (Vol. VII). Minneapolis: Harrison and Smith State Printers, 1893: **196**, **201**, **202**, **206**, **207**, **215**.

The photos on the following pages originate from Jacob Brower's *Itasca State Park: An Illustrated History*, Minnesota Historical Collections (Vol. XI). St. Paul: Minnesota Historical Society, 1904: **220** (both), **225, 242**.

All other photos by Deane Johnson.

About the Author

Deane Johnson has been an active photographer since acquiring his first Canon FTb in 1976. He grew up in Grand Forks, ND, and has lived and traveled throughout northern Minnesota. Drawn to the lakes and woods of Park Rapids, MN, in 1980, he has lived there since then. A retired family physician, he was a founding member of the Jackpine Writers' Bloc, plays clarinet and saxophone, and was a co-owner of Beagle Books of Park Rapids with his wife, Jill. He was the photographer for Jill's book, *Little Minnesota: 100 Towns Around 100*.